D1249425

Victorian Style

John Crosby Freeman

Victorian Style

An Alphabetical Compendium of Design, Crafts, Ideas, and More

Stoddart

A TERN ENTERPRISE BOOK

First published in 1991 by
Stoddart Publishing Co. Limited
34 Lesmill Road
Toronto, Canada
M3B 2T6

Canadian Cataloguing-in-Publication Data
Freeman, John C. (John Crosby)
Victorian style

ISBN 0-7737-2459-1

1. Decorative arts, Victorian. 2. Decoration and ornament—Victorian style. 3. Interior decoration. I. Title.

NK2115.V53F73 749.2'04 C91-093474-6

VICTORIAN STYLE
An Alphabetical Compendium of Design, Crafts, Ideas, and More
was prepared and produced by
Tern Enterprise, Inc.
15 West 26th Street
New York, New York 10010

Designer: Devorah Levinrad
Display Typography: Stephanie Bart-Horvath
Photography Editor: Ede Rothaus

Typeset by Bookworks Plus

Printed and bound in Hong Kong by Leefung-Asco Printers, Ltd.

To the gentlemen, especially Graydon La Verne (Larry) Freeman, my father, who is now in his eighty-seventh year of life. Thanks to him, I grew up surrounded by Victoriana and acquired his affection for it. More a cultural historian than a connoisseur, he was instinctively more protective of common artifacts used by many people than rare objects used by few. Long before Victoriana was fashionable, I often heard him say, "If I don't take it home now, who will save it for tomorrow?" That's why I think of him as one of the Salvation Army of Victoriana, "loving the unlovable."

Table of

THE BLACK PRINCE

THE
"WALTER CRANE
WALL PAPERS"
JEFFREY & CO.,
64, ESSEX ROAD, N.

Contents

The Victorian Revival

Victorian is now well-established in the aristocracy of period styles and admired by design scholars and amateur decorators alike. But from 1930 to 1980, this style was considered odd, clunky, and outdated, and anyone in the trend-conscious worlds of art and scholarship who admired it was looked at askance.

Pioneers of the Victorian Revival during those fifty years could tell stories that reveal the magnitude of distaste for Victoriana. Samuel J. Dornsife is now a senior restorer of Victorian interiors. In the 1930s, he was a young, second-generation interior decorator. At a country sale, after he successfully bid on a suite of ornate Victorian Belter furniture, the auctioneer pointed at him and yelled, "Stand up kid!" He stood up. To the crowd the auctioneer said, "I want everyone to see the damned fool who just bought this junk!" John Maass is now a senior historian of Victorian architecture. In 1957, *Time* magazine gave his first book, *The Gingerbread Age,* a man-bites-dog review because it seemed odd for an architectural historian to be enthusiastic about Victorian buildings.

When the Victorian Revival began in earnest in the 1980s, it was due to the perseverance of these and other artists and scholars, as well as the popular media, which patiently refused to ignore this romantic era. On Broadway, in 1935, Queen Victoria was humanized in *Victoria Regina*—a production that provided its Queen Victoria (Helen Hayes) with a permanent private persona and its Prince Albert (Vincent Price) with a permanent career change from architecture to acting. Victorian was resplendent in movie versions of historical fiction like *Gone With the Wind* and countless Westerns. In the 1970s, the residences of TV situation comedies, such as "The Mary Tyler Moore Show" and "Mork and Mindy," were Queen Anne houses, highlighting the charming possibilities of these unpopular structures.

At this time, people rediscovered the allure of Victorian buildings. This was a terrific opportunity, for many people were already living in towns and cities founded or developed during the Victorian

A portrait of Her Majesty, Victoria, by A. Duduzeau, presented on Sèvres china.

period. After the turbulent 1960s and uncertain 1970s, they were drawn to the stability of the past, embodied in the grace of Victorian structures. Besides, they were often bargains compared with the prices of new, considerably less charming buildings. People had tired of the clean—and some would say boring—lines of contemporary buildings and furniture. They craved more detail and ornamentation in their homes, as in the buildings of the Victorian era.

The world-wide prestige of the British Empire during Queen Victoria's long reign—from 1837 until her death in 1901—made it convenient for English-speaking historians to call a big chunk of the nineteenth century the Victorian period. But there was confusion in the convenience when it came to sorting out the facts, especially about the matter that concerns us most—*style.* To put it bluntly, Victorian was not a style; it was a period of multiple styles in transition.

Andrew Jackson Downing—the landscape designer and advocate of the rustic cottage home—is often credited with initiating a number of Victorian architectural styles when he attacked the popularity of Greek Revival houses in the 1840s. But the fundamental princi-

Virginia State Capitol, Richmond, Virginia.

ple of Victorian styles was born in the 1780s in America when Thomas Jefferson invented the first architecture of historic associations. After the capital of Virginia was moved in 1780 from Williamsburg to Richmond, Jefferson designed the new State Capitol as an imitation of a temple built during the Ancient Roman Republic.

Despite Downing's diatribe against Greek Revival style, it remained popular from its beginnings in 1800 through Downing's lifetime and after his death in 1852. Don't let Downing keep the Victorian lover in you away from the simplicity and economy of a Greek Revival house. With landscaping and interiors done in any Victorian style you choose, it could be the perfect compromise between the old tradition of neoclassicism and the revived tradition of Victorianism. There's nothing new about combining neoclassicism and Victorianism. If you study Victorian homes with a cool head you'll discover that most of them are central-entrance, classical vernacular boxes of Federal or Greek Revival proportions enriched by the ornamental overlays characteristic of their nominal Victorian style.

Many examples of Victorian-era structures exist today, and aspiring homeowners can select from a variety of styles. One reason that

Queen Anne mansions became popular during the 1980s is that their design ethic of "more is more" appealed to the upwardly mobile, conspicuous consumption of two-income young professionals. For those whose tastes are less elaborate, more modest options are the cottage and villa styles. They tend to be more personally satisfying to renovate and decorate because they require less professional help. Of course, this book illustrates some grande dames of Victorian exterior and interior mansion decoration, but the majority of photographs depict more economical examples of Victorian villa and cottage lifestyles.

Victorian stylebooks rarely said that elaborately scaled and expensively furnished homes were inherently superior. Today, as home ownership has become increasingly difficult, it makes sense to adopt the Victorian attitude of being grateful for any kind of home one can call "my own." If a Victorian cottage is all that you can afford, do the best you can with your resources. The result will be as charming as the villa or mansion efforts of persons with ten to a hundred times more money, because you have done so much of it yourself.

Victorian cottages are the most accessible of nineteenth-century types because the appropriate furnishings for them are inexpensive. Nowadays, many of these items refer to the style of furnishings called Country.

Victorian identity was the kiss of death to Victorian cottage antiques during the dark decades of the Victorian Revival. Most of the time it was sold as Folk Art, but a clever marketing ploy during the 1970s altered its image into Country.

The distinction was between "good" Country and "bad" Victorian. Country was simple, naive, and restrained in its use of ornament. Victorian was excessively complex and ornate. Country used solid native woods with natural finishes. Victorian used foreign woods, veneers, stains, and varnishes. Country colors were flat and muted. Victorian colors were glossy and bright. Country styles were homemade. Victorian styles were imported. Country was fun. Victorian was serious. It's time to put an end to this persiflage. Anything made between 1837–1901 is Victorian. Anything in a Victorian mode from the end of this period to the 1920s is *Victorian Survival.* Anything in a Victorian mode after 1930 is *Victorian Revival.*

It's easy to transform Country into Victorian Cottage. Banish the decorated milk-cans, painted chicken crates, horse collar mirrors, pitchforks, and other barnyard antiques. Donate the bears,

Abraham Lincoln's bedroom, Springfield, Illinois, lacks the clutter commonly associated with Victorian interiors. That is less surprising to common misconceptions of Victorian interior decoration than the collision of colors and patterns on the walls and floor.

geese, and ducks to someone else's zoo. Cut the collection of heart shapes by two-thirds, if not altogether. These objects have little to do with a proper Victorian interior.

Victorians weren't opposed to the inclusion of obsolete objects in rooms. For example, after the Colonial tall-case clock in the parlor was made obsolete by mass-produced Victorian shelf-clocks, it was romanticized and relocated in 1843 by Henry Wadsworth Longfellow's *The Old Clock on the Stairs.* It has been called a "grandfather clock" since 1876 when a popular song of that name by Henry Clay Work was published to coincide with the Centennial Exhibition in Philadelphia. From then to this day, no Colonial Revival home would be considered truly complete without a reproduction or antique grandfather clock somewhere in the vicinity of the stairs.

Victorians were opposed to using obsolete objects in inappropriate ways. For example, they would never have decorated their parlors and dining rooms with items meant to be placed in kitchens, bedrooms, and bathrooms. Avoid embarrassing situations like the one told me by a Chinese scholar who was invited to a fancy dinner party at the home of a prominent Los Angeles collector of oriental ceramics. He nearly gagged during the soup course, but quickly regained his composure when he realized he was the only person in the room who knew the magnificent celadon tureen was originally a royal chamber pot.

Some Victoriana lovers feel guilty about having modern appliances in their rooms. Therefore, they conceal these items behind cupboards, closets, and armoires. There's nothing strange about parking contemporary automobiles outside Victorian homes, so nobody should feel uncomfortable about having today's household appliances inside Victorian homes.

Late Victorian designers took adolescent pleasure in reshaping the classical language of architecture to their own expressive purposes.

Although the Victorians bequeathed the period room concept to us via their charming stylebooks and delightful catalogs of merchandise, the majority of Victorians didn't live in period rooms. Drawings, prints, paintings, magazine illustrations, and photographs reveal that most Victorians furnished their interiors with new and old things made in a variety of styles. It's certainly possible to create period rooms filled only with Victorian objects. But if you want your Victorian Revival home to be both comfortable and practical—the goal of most Victorians—then you should feel free to mix romantic artifacts of different vintages and styles with harmonious colors.

Victorian life was a smorgasbord existence; there was so much to choose from at any given time. That's why I've arranged this book like a buffet. There are no rambling, episodic chapters telling you all you need to know about every period or every style, only a richly varied menu from A to Z of accessible Victoriana. Welcome to the feast. I hope you enjoy consuming it as much as I did putting it together.

Architectural Styles

The typical *Gothic Revival* house was a one-story rural *cottage.* It was philosophically appealing to parsons, artists, authors, and other members of the genteel poor as well as Early Victorian scientific farmers. A few large ones were built, but they were exceptional, and those that survive are curiosities.

The typical *Italianate* house was a two-story suburban *villa.* It was the home of the solid middle class—shop- and factory-owners, lawyers, and merchants. It was possible to enlarge or diminish them, but their true position in the architectural scheme was middling.

This mansardic design was the frontispiece for A. J. Bicknell's Village Builder Supplement of 1871.

The typical *Mansardic* house was a three-story urban *mansion.* Inspired by a seventeenth-century urban style revived for the rebuilding of Paris during the Second Empire of Louis Napoleon in the 1850s and 1860s, this Victorian style carried urban and civic associations. These were the homes of the plutocracy as well as the buildings that served as High Victorian post offices, city halls, court houses, and high schools. Patternbooks of the period had designs for houses of one story plus mansard roof, but they looked like amputees.

There was no typical *Queen Anne* house. It could appear cheap or expensive, simple or complex. Such homes were built in rural, suburban, and urban areas and could take the form of cottages, villas, or mansions. Memorable ones featured lavish displays of ornamentation within a symphony of materials and textures. Forms were whimsically pilfered from the bazaar of world architectural history and boldly painted in several secondary and tertiary colors. The multiplicity and exuberant vitality of the Queen Anne distinguishes it from the singularity and controlled strength of earlier Victorian styles. For those acquiring a taste for them, they are like good, but idiosyncratic, friends.

Queen Anne must have plenty of friends today because most Americans have fixed it in their minds as the quintessential Victorian style to the exclusion of all other forms of Victorian romanticism that preceded or followed it.

Queen Anne houses built in the late nineteenth century revelled in architectural details from different historic styles. They also displayed a variety of surface textures.

One day a lady telephoned with an architectural query about her old farmhouse in Illinois. She apologized for bothering me about a house that wasn't Victorian. I asked her, "When was it built?" She replied, "1860." "Does it have cornice brackets?" "Yes." "Does it have a verandah?" "Yes." "Does it have bay windows?" "Yes, two of them." "My dear lady," I said. "You don't have a Queen Anne house, but it's Victorian for sure!"

Queen Anne is remembered today more than any other Victorian style because it lacked institutional associations and singular historic references. Unlike neoclassical designs, it did not carry a symbolic message and was meant to be appreciated for its looks alone. It was not a profound style, but one that allowed great leeway in choices of materials, colors, and finishes. From 1880 until the devastating world-wide depression of 1893, Queen Anne supplied a style for the "Victorian Happy Days" that was genial, generous, and romantic. It survived in the imagination of American popular culture because it was accessible, and still is, to an immense number of people.

ART: SELF-TAUGHT

Few self-taught artists ever supported a studio like this one, owned by successful landscape painter Frederic Church in his home at Olana, New York, overlooking the Hudson River. Note the Pompeiian red wall color.

The ability of a woman to create something with her hands beyond obligatory needlecraft was highly honored during the Victorian period. Although it doesn't sound like much today, being "an accomplished lady" was the brightest jewel in the crown of any Victorian woman, even if it only amounted to a few theorem paintings on velvet.

Victorian cities had established schools and academies where the fine arts were taught. Victorian villages depended upon itinerants and resident "accomplished ladies" to create attractive artwork for local homes. But the majority of Victorian women were self-taught from books of art instruction, many published by Victorian manufacturers of art supplies like Windsor and Newton. "Drawing Cards" were published as models for copying; it is from these that today's crayon books for children descended. Such art instruction was a staple of Victorian ladies' magazines published by Godey, Peterson, Graham, and Leslie.

You can color prints taken from Victorian illustrated periodicals like *Harper's Weekly.* Before you ruin a real piece of Victoriana, hone your water-coloring skills on scrap pictures. Also study originals—most of which were rapidly executed by small armies of poorly paid women working piece rate. Also keep in mind that broad areas of grayed colors surrounding a splash or two of red goes a long way. Avoid overworking and overcoloring your pictures. (*See also Ceramics*)

Further Reading: Drepperd, Carl. *American Pioneer Arts & Artists* (Watkins Glen, NY: American Life Books, 1970). An informative guide with a 26-page chapter and bibliography on "Art Instruction Books for the American People."

Bathrooms

Late Victorians encased their bathroom implements and fixtures in familiar furniture forms. They decorated their bathrooms with the same level of formality as adjacent bedrooms. When creating a Victorian Revival bathroom, avoid overuse of architectural salvage materials, especially overscaled stained glass windows from early twentieth-century churches. Period illustrations, taken from Victorian plumbing catalogs, can help you create an authentic interior.

Elizabethan Bathroom: It's possible to recreate this bathroom without spending a fortune simply by taking away the columns on the encased toilet, tub, sitz bath, bidet, and lavatory. You could tile the walls up to a wallpapered or stenciled border. Simple moldings over the joints in a plasterboard ceiling could be extended down the end wall to frame the window. As a final flourish, place oriental rugs on a prefabricated parquet floor and some framed pictures on the wall.

All bathroom fixtures shown in this 1888 plumbing catalogue have been encased in the Late Victorian Elizabethan style appropriate for a Queen Anne style mansion.

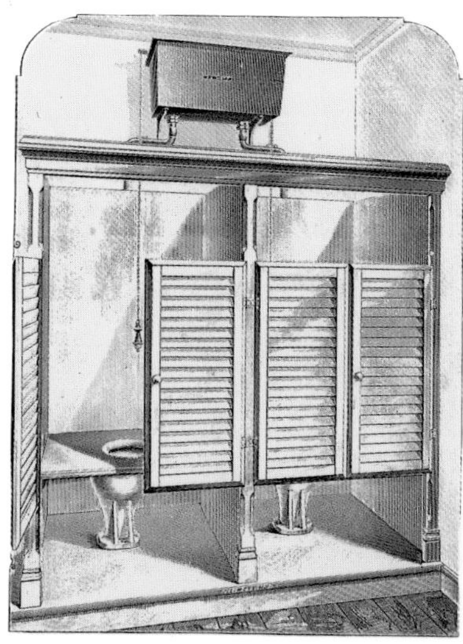

Interior blinds can be used to Victorianize one or two regular toilets, like this one from the 1888 Mott plumbing catalogue.

This 13 x 10½-foot (4 x 3.2 m) interior is arranged to provide a clear passage and central axis from the door to the window. The focal point of this bathroom is not the furniture but the drapery, window, and decoration on the walls.

Half-Circle Wash Stand: The cast-iron half-circle wash stand in the Italianate style from Mott's 1888 plumbing catalog is a survivor from the days of Early Victorian personal hygiene. It's a glorified washbowl-and-pitcher set with storage space for a chamber pot. Mott converted it to plumbing by providing two faucet holes, but it could be ordered without them. The fixture was supplied "Plain, Painted, Galvanized or Marbleized." Today, it's a practical reminder that any case piece of Victorian furniture in the right size can be converted into an authentic Victorian lavatory.

Open Recessed Lavatory: Late Victorians of advanced sensibilities could "meet the prevailing demand for fine plumbing appliances adapted to being fitted up without being encased" with Mott's Open Lavatories. This one is cleverly encased in the space of a recess decorated by an architrave of decorated tiles.

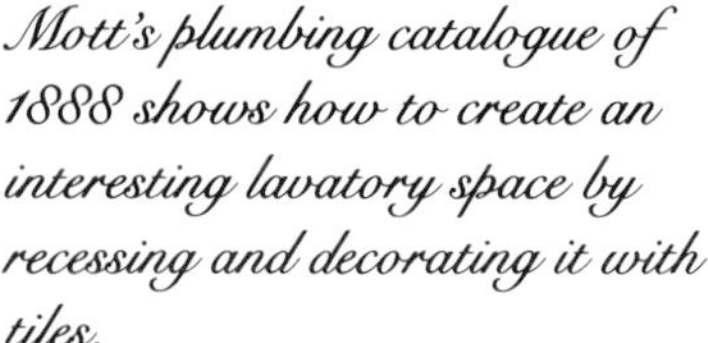

Mott's plumbing catalogue of 1888 shows how to create an interesting lavatory space by recessing and decorating it with tiles.

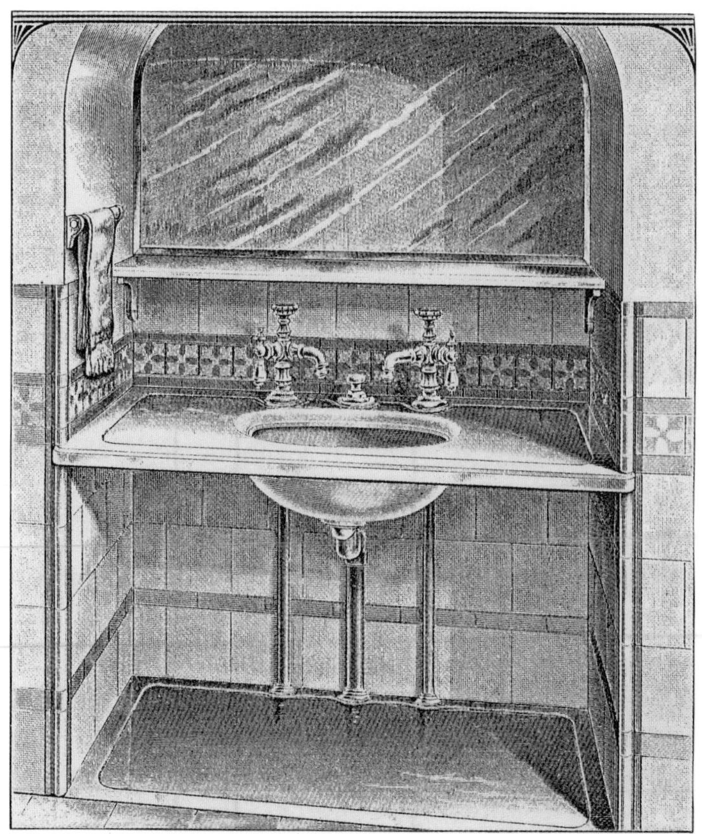

Hand-painted borders, like these from a 1900 plumbing catalogue, beautified plain white tubs.

Toilet: Any basic toilet can be Victorianized by an "open seat." It could be made today by simple joinery and a pair of salvaged chair legs.

Closet Toilet: Mott shows a way to finesse the pull-chain furor of today's Victorian Revival—simply closet one or two regular toilets behind doors or blinds.

Bathtub: By 1900, encased bathroom fixtures had virtually disappeared from the marketplace. There were none in Wolff's 1900 catalog, which showed sleek modern units like "*Lethean* Bath Finished Zinc White outside, with two Gold Bands." Persons requiring an extra jolt in the morning could brave the thrill of Wolff's "Needle Bath with Overhead Shower."

Simple cabinetry is all it takes to convert any basic bathtub into an elegant Victorian fixture. Mott supplied it in cherry, black walnut, or ash.

Hand Painted Borders: For an extra $6.25 to $25 Wolff would provide its tubs with pretty hand-painted borders like these above. If you want to beautify your plain white tub with an authentic Victorian form of decoration, this example might inspire you.

Victorian plumbing, represented by the lavatory in the foreground, made the Victorian washstand, with its pitcher and bowl, obsolete. But washstands and their accessories continued to be made and used well into the twentieth century, because indoor plumbing was installed in more villas and mansions than cottages.

Bedrooms

Bedrooms are the least public and most romantic rooms in a home. Since it's the one room most folks want to see, the bugaboo of public performance raises its anxious head once again.

Just as it is possible to have a Victorian dining room without a Victorian dining table, you can have a Victorian bedroom without a Victorian bed. This relieves you from the expense and size limitations of the real thing and allows you to rest in the style you prefer, as long as it does not obviously clash with your decor.

There is no rule that says a Victorian bedroom has to have a bed with a footboard unless you want one. By shifting the emphasis from the bedframe to the bedcovering, which can be a colorful quilt, the bed area is appropriately emphasized. (*See also Quilts*)

You can create an elegant focal point in a Victorian bedroom

A corona, which might be found over a Victorian bedstead, has migrated to the wall above the vanity table, which is an excellent example of how fabrics can be used to convert plain pieces into romantic furniture. In the midst of so much colored pattern, the white bedspread and pillow-shams provide a pleasant oasis.

with a half-tester canopy at the back of the bed or a corona suspended from the ceiling over the center of the bed. Scale the half-tester or corona in proportion to the the size of the mattress. This is much preferred to attaching an old, full-size headboard to the wall behind a bigger, modern bed.

Victorians often decorated bedrooms with light and cool colors, small-scale prints, and upholstered furniture. Depending on your space and budget, you can create anything between a cottage and a baronial boudoir/salon. Most will be content simply to make the area cozy, and that's Victorian too.

The biggest drawback to an old Victorian bedroom is the lack of closet space, something quickly but no longer cheaply solved in the Victorian manner with free-standing closets called wardrobes or armoires. A pair of antique doors or new ones in an antique style could be made by a cabinetmaker into a wardrobe built into the corner, thereby eliminating the expense of the backing and one of the sides. If space allows, you might position one on the wall containing the bathroom for a washer and dryer, balancing it with another on the opposite side. The cheapest and most decorative solution would be folding screens.

Victorians had wall-to-wall carpets, but they weren't solid color deep-pile like those of today. If your bedroom already has modern wall-to-wall, you could artfully scatter oriental rugs to define areas, paths, and generally break up the floor space. Or you could trim away the perimeter to reveal a wide border of natural wood floor. (*See also Rugs and Carpets*)

If the woodwork of the window casings is attractive, it is a needless expense to obscure it with heavy drapery when light-colored net or lace panels will satisfy the requirement just as well. Hang them within the sash area and loop them back to the jambs with decorative tie-backs. Quilted roller shades could be a handsome and practical addition to the panels. (*See also Fabrics, Lace, Roller Shades, Screens*)

Berlin Work and Samplers

Victorian home-made decorative art was an elaborate and deliberate system to imprison Victorian women of intelligence, talent, and leisure in pretty but petty exercises that kept them occupied and away from the male-dominated Victorian world of real work. If this statement was absolutely true, home-made decorative arts would, by now, have ceased to exist. However, if a Victorian woman could be transported by a time machine into a contemporary craft shop, she would see much that was familiar.

Of all the Victorian needlework craft projects, counted-stitch wool- or worsted-work was the most popular. Today, it is better known as petit-point or needlepoint, but when German printers in Berlin flooded the Victorian world with their colored patterns on squared paper Victorians called it "Berlin Work."

No images were too complicated for Berlin Work: fruits and flowers, pets and other animals, heads of people and full-length portaits—even famous paintings by Victorian or Renaissance artists. Much time and talent was concentrated by Victorian ladies into their Berlin Work, giving it an intensity of effort rarely equalled today. Francis Lichten, writing in 1950, said, "Today few do more

The lambrequin was based on a Berlin work pattern. It probably hung over and decorated the edge of a small shelf for a shelf clock. (See page 45 for another example of a Berlin work lambrequin.)

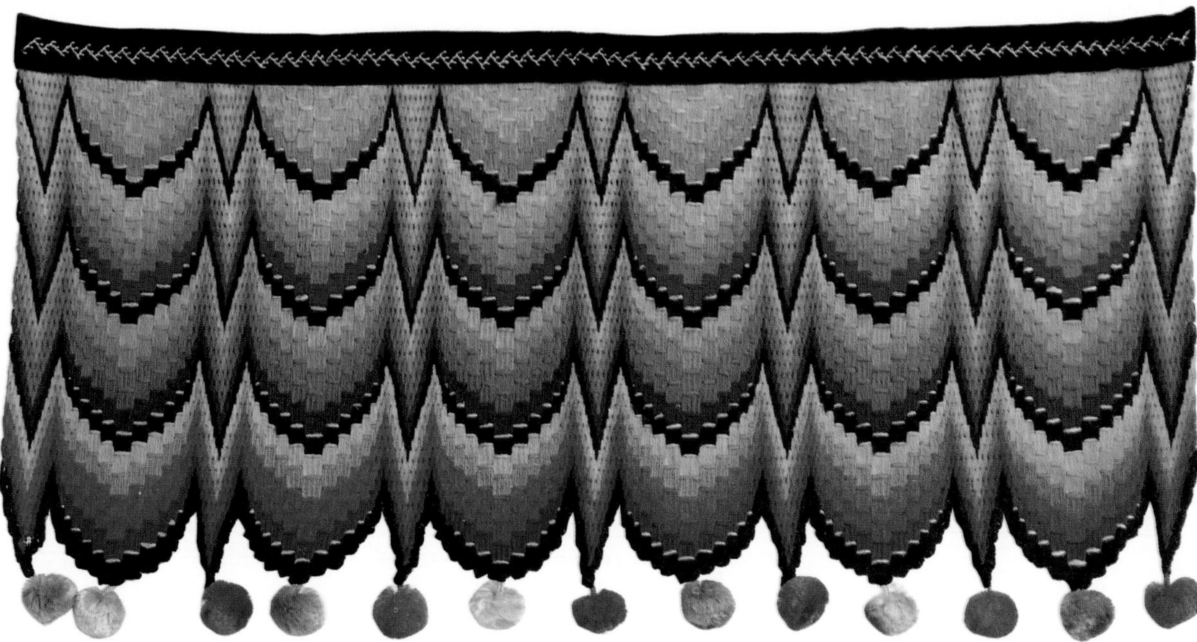

than fill in backgrounds on pieces imported with the ornamental details completely worked out. Nineteenth-century needlewomen who vaunted themselves on their ability to execute subjects of the greatest intricacy would be apt to regard the achievements of their descendants as evidence of sad incompetency."

Further Reading: Lichten, Frances. *Decorative Art of Victoria's Era* (New York: Charles Scribner's Sons, 1950).

For those who could afford it, a billiard table was a Victorian family home entertainment center.

BILLIARD ROOM

Billiards was not a game played exclusively by gentlemen—although contemporary movies with Victorian and Edwardian settings reinforce this misconception. Despite the sexist denomination of Victorian rooms like the dining room as male and the parlor as female, there was nothing to stop great-grandmama from "shooting pool." Decorous deployment of the bridge made it possible for her to avoid mounting the table for tricky shots.

The early history of billiards is delightfully mixed up with shuffleboard, pall-mall, croquet, and a form of miniature golf. By the seventeenth century it was well established as a table game played with balls and maces. By 1800 the more elegant and accurate cue stick with leather tip had replaced the crude mace. Vulcanized rubber replaced felt cushions in the late 1840s. The first patent for modern composition balls was in 1880, but ivory balls were used throughout the nineteenth century.

Billiards, in all of its varieties, is currently enjoying a well-deserved revival. It is easy to learn and can be played by anyone capable of raising a cue stick off the table surface. If a Victorian billiard room is to be a serious part of your new or old Victorian home, down in the basement or out in the garage is not a proper location.

The younger generation is enjoying "a bit of a lark" cavorting around and on the family billiard table.

Brackets and Bargeboards

Neoclassical brackets and Gothic Revival bargeboards are the chief forms of architectural detail giving style to Victorian buildings. Architectural historians of the Modern School criticized ornamentation because it didn't serve structural purposes. However, no architectural book of the Victorian period ever claimed such details were structural. Their function was to provide visual strength and enrichment to cornices. Late Victorian millwork catalogs sometimes called brackets and bargeboards "cornice drapery," thereby revealing the Victorian penchant for exteriorizing interior decoration.

White paint has been recently applied so that the brackets of this wonderful Italianate cornice appear isolated, though they are more obvious as an example here. Victorians used colors to integrate architectural details and would have painted these a more harmonious color.

Local builders often kept busy during the winter months manufacturing architectural details in their backyard shops. Beginning about 1870, local millwork companies started supplying nationally standardized designs and molding profiles in addition to custom orders. As late as 1918, Early Victorian brackets and bargeboards were still being illustrated in Hodgson's *Modern Carpentry* "to give the workman an idea of the shape and construction of low-cost ornamental wood-work."

Most contemporary designers of Victorian Revival homes don't know how to ornamentalize and enrich cornices. They could learn plenty if they would study local examples of the real thing. The problem lies in their ignorance of Victorian brackets and bargeboards as a *system* of ornament.

The neoclassical system of architectural orders was the instructional base of self-taught builders and professionally trained architects. From it they learned that brackets were not isolated bits of "gingerbread" stuck on to spice up rooflines. They were integral parts of the classical *entablature* with its horizontal elements of upper *cornice,* middle *frieze,* and lower *architrave.* Although the vertical

Elaborate brackets in the cornices of a Late Victorian Italianate commercial building in Ferndale, California, create magnificent crowns for bay windows.

brackets were never named for the Ancient *triglyphs* or beam-ends of the Doric Order which they emulate, a horizontal band of tooth-like brackets at the top of a frieze board was and still is called by its neoclassical name, *dentils.*

Victorian neoclassical cornices were rarely slavish copies of ancient examples. Architectural practice is like learning any language—a set of relationships that, once mastered, can be altered to create dramatic accents. Once Victorian cornices are studied on their own terms, they can be appreciated for what they always were —Victorian architectural special effects.

Bargeboards as surrogates for the collective Victorian subconscious were put on the couch for Freudian analysis in a book by Ben Karp with the predictable result that any ornamental feature which protruded, dangled, or profiled in a suggestive pattern revealed deep, dark secrets about Victorian sexuality.

Further Reading: Karp, Ben. *Wood Motifs in American Domestic Architecture* (New York: A.S. Barnes, 1966).

Built-in Furniture

Built-in furniture is commonly associated with styles sandwiching the Victorian period—Early American corner cupboards and Mission sideboards. The corner cupboard remained a popular piece for Victorian cottages well into the nineteenth century. Like other types of built-in furniture, the corner cupboard has both economic and aesthetic benefits. It eliminates the expense of a back and sides, and it is cheaper to build it on site than buy it from a shop or manufacturer's catalog. Adjusting the scale of the piece to the room and integrating the woodwork of the room with the woodwork of the furniture is easier, also. Victorian kitchens and pantries almost always had built-in furniture. Queen Anne interiors at every level often featured built-in nooks, window seats, sideboards, and china cabinets.

Victorian Revival interiors especially benefit from built-in furniture for the same reasons it was made in the first place. It allows interiors to be customized. New or old doors, hardware, moldings, paneling, and decorative glass can be transformed by basic cabinetry skills into impressive and elegant Victorian-style pieces.

Early twentieth-century interiors like this kitchen continued the Victorian tradition of built-in furniture.

Ceilings

"If one part only can be decorated, let that one part be the ceiling," wrote Christopher Dresser in *Principles of Decorative Design* (1873). "Our ceilings, which can be properly seen, are usually white in middle-class houses. Why not have beautiful ceilings, especially as they can be seen complete, while the wall is part hidden by furniture and pictures?"

Dresser sought to beautify ceilings primarily through painting them. A conservative formula is to use a solid color three tints lighter than the color of the walls. Cream, pale blue, or a pale ultramarine grayed with raw umber were recommended by Dresser. Stenciling "simple patterns in cream-color on blue ground, but having a black outline, also look well; and these might be prepared on paper, and hung on the ceiling as common paper-hangings." Dresser also recommended "gold ornaments on a deep blue ground, with black outline," for their rich effect.

Embossed tin ceilings were an economical and durable alternative to painted, stenciled, or wall-papered ceilings.

Dresser despised plaster centerpieces, also called rosettes, flowers, and medallions. With or without simple borders in plaster or paint along the edges of the ceiling, centerpieces were used thoughout the Victorian period and for many satisfied the requirement of a decorated ceiling. If you don't have a lighting fixture to hang from a centerpiece, heed Dresser's advice and do without.

Dresser, like other advanced designers of his time, had a simple reverence for the "reality" of decorated surfaces. If a ceiling was flat, then the ceiling's ornamentation should be flat. "All fictitious appearance of relief must be avoided. What can be worse than festoons of leafage, like so many sausages, painted upon a ceiling, with griffins, small framed pictures, impossible flowers, all with fictitious light and shade?" If that's what you want on your ceiling, however, don't let Dresser stop you. But that kind of ceiling, when it is supported by appropriate wall and window treatments, is more expensive and difficult to do successfully than what Dresser recommends.

If you wish to decorate your ceilings, scan Victorian Revival catalogs of tin ceilings, embossed Anaglypta, plaster ornaments, stencils, and ceiling papers. Resist the temptation to over-decorate the ceiling, however. Dresser advised, "A ceiling should be beautiful, and should also be manifest," but it shouldn't look like a fantastic flying carpet hovering oppressively over the space below.

Stained-glass ceilings were associated with houses in the mansion class, and with civic buildings such as capitols and courthouses.

Ceramics

Ceramics, sometimes spelled by Victorians in the affected Greek manner "Keramics," was the wedge that opened Victorian museums of fine art to the decorative arts. It couldn't be denied that ceramics were major art forms for the Ancient Greeks, Persians, Chinese, Japanese, and Koreans. But with the ambitious arrogance typical of the time, Victorian art potters believed they could achieve for their own work the same exhalted status. Outside serious aesthetic circles this amounted to a running joke called "Chinamania" —the purchase of new and old pottery at exorbitant rates. The most famous was duMaurier's cartoon for *Punch* showing an emaciated couple dressed in the Aesthetic mode stunned in the presence of their most recent purchase of old cracked china and wondering, "Can we live up to it?"

Ceramics as fine art energized the creation of the most pretentious pottery of the period, including the vulgar Late Victorian

Blue-and-white transfer-painted wares were a perennial Victorian favorite for cottage kitchens.

majolica, justified by its references to Renaissance Italian tin-glazed wares that have enjoyed a new vogue as a collectible in the 1980s. Even the ugliest examples of Victorian art pottery are avidly collected today.

Hand-painted china deserves special mention because it has survived and continues to thrive in the late twentieth century in the same manner that it did in the nineteenth—as an art form for amateurs. Today's hobby ceramicists would get more pleasing benefits

if they would take the time to study the ample sources of designs in Victorian guidebooks and patternbooks, as well as surviving examples of the art. A good place to start is with three books by M. Louise McLaughlin, who is said to be the pioneer of china painting in America.

If the process of finding, framing, and placing prints and paints on your walls makes you uncomfortable and is beyond your means, consider the Victorian tradition of decorating with ceramics. If you are decorating in the Victorian cottage style, a collection of figural pottery would be appropriate. Otherwise you can hang your most magnificent platters on the walls, line up your prettiest plates on the plate rails, and arrange your cups and jugs in the china cabinet.

In the pursuit of authentic Victorian colors one source that has not faded with time is Victorian ceramics. If you want to know the popular colors of any period, study its ceramics. (*See also Tiles*)

Further Reading: Edwin Atlee Barber. *Pottery and Porcelain of the United States* (Watkins Glen, NY: American Life Books). This is the standard Victorian history, first published in 1893, now available in an excellent amended facsimile. McLaughlin, M. Louise. *China Painting* (1877), *Pottery Decoration Under the Glaze* (1880), and *Suggestions to China Painters* (1890).

CHAIRS

No single type of furniture reveals the ingenuity and diversity of the Victorian decorative arts better than chairs. Victorians made chairs for every season, for every reason, and with any material capable of doing the job.

Chairs were the first mass-produced type of furniture and probably the first furniture shipped outside local markets "K.D."—

King was proud of the medal it won at the 1853 New York Crystal Palace Exhibition. With the exception of the invalid chair in the lower right, all the chairs were designed for male occupants. The armchair was a traditional male prerogative that Victorian society perpetuated. Victorian women couldn't fit in them even if they wanted to, because the skirts of the 1850s fanned out with layers of crinoline underskirts.

knocked down. There were so many Victorian chair makers because demand was great, entry-level skills were sufficient for the lower end of the market, and it required little machinery to get started. Gustav Stickley, the famous manufacturer of Edwardian Arts & Crafts furniture in the Craftsman Mission style, began his Late Victorian career in his uncle's chair shop. Its output was simple "stick" chairs. Even big and highly mechanized fancy furniture

manufacturers had bread-and-butter lines of cheap chairs for homes, offices, and hotels.

Those on a tight budget may despair of owning a Victorian dining table, china cabinet, sideboard, or bedstead. But they can still find reasonably priced Victorian chairs in abundance. Visit any second-hand store from antiques galleries down to junk shops. Somewhere you will find them—chairs lined in rows, chairs heaped in piles, chairs skied to the rafters on pegs or nails.

Don't shun common Victorian chairs, even if they are mismatched. In parlors they can be unified by matching cushions. In dining rooms they can be matched by putting drawstring bags with the same pattern over the backs. You won't have to use that subterfuge if you can find pairs of each type and arrange them symmetrically around the table, placing a matched or similar pair of arm chairs at the heads of the table.

Don't shun Victorian chairs in need of reupholstering, either. It will take some time to locate the appropriate fabrics and decorations as well as learn how to do it yourself or find someone to do it for you, but in the process of such hand-to-hand combat you will learn the biography of your chair—where its components came from, the people who might have manufactured it, the people who might have used it, and the decade in which it was made.

Damask fabric, buttoned and tuffed, is the quintessential Mid-Victorian upholstery.

Chromolithographs

The controversial chromolithograph was the brainchild of a German immigrant named Louis Prang. "Prang's American Chromos are facsimile reproductions of masterly oil and water-color paintings, so skillfully and artistically done that it requires the experience of an expert to detect the difference between them and their originals," said the first issue of *Prang's Chromo* published in Boston in January 1868.

Prang's reproductions in color of the world's fine art failed to find their way beyond the walls of middle-class parlors. They were too expensive for those in lower classes. The upper classes could afford original fine art prints and paintings. Although Prang helped many living Victorian artists by purchasing and reproducing their works, he was a convenient target for the criticisms of Victorian fine art purists blinded by their fears of substituting reproductions for the real thing. They failed to see his primary objective was art education—a movement that he fostered in America. Prang is still maintained as a registered trademark for art education materials by the Dixon Ticonderoga Company of Sandusky, Ohio.

Framed like easel paintings and marked on the back, Prang's Chromos were never sold as anything but reproductions. Today they are scarce because so few were made relative to the output of the more popular hand-colored lithographs of Currier & Ives. Most were doomed to destruction by their framing as easel paintings. During the dark decades of the Victorian Revival in the twentieth century, when anything Late Victorian was regarded as the epitome of ugliness, they fell prey to people who decided fine art frames were worth more than fine art reproductions. More difficult to store than flat prints, they were eventually damaged and thrown away.

Prang was also the father of the American greeting card industry, particularly Christmas cards. Beginning in 1880, he arranged competitive exhibitions of artwork for Christmas cards by American artists with the inducement of big money prizes awarded to the four

"Neptune's Horses" by Walter Crane, a first sketch exhibited at the Royal Water Colour Society in 1872 and reproduced in The Easter Art Annual in 1898.

best designs. The judges were: Samuel Colman, a partner in the Aesthetic Movement decorating firm of Associated Artists; Richard Morris Hunt, the Beaux-Arts architect; and E.C. Moore, head of the silver department at Tiffany's. For the third competition of 1882, Prang added a second group of public prizes to be awarded by popular ballot. The voting artists and the voting visitors gave first prize to Dora Wheeler, youngest daughter of Associated Artists partner Candace Wheeler.

Further Reading: Freeman, Larry. *Louis Prang: Color Lithographer* (Watkins Glen, NY: Century House, 1971). Available from American Life Books.

Clothing

If you are tempted to dress up for some Victorian event in your home or community, a few facts of life stand in the way of your achieving perfect verisimilitude. A visit to the nearest costume collection or special exhibitions like The Brooklyn Museum's recent show on the great Victorian designer Charles Worth will reveal the problem of *scale.* During a century or more of better medicine and nutrition most of us have grown taller than our Victorian ancestors. Unless you have been blessed with a Victorian physique, don't bother with antique Victorian clothing.

Victorian women of fashion dressed like priests fully vested for high holy days—most apparel was heavy, hot, and uncomfortable.

Victorian clothing, especially women's, is a desirable collectible today.

One only has to recall the scene in *Gone With the Wind* in which Scarlett O'Hara is laced into tight undergarments, clutching the bedpost like Odysseus during the storm, and it becomes clear why Victorian women frequently fainted.

Instead of fitting yourself into old Victorian clothing and straining both you and the clothing needlessly, it's more practical to emulate Victorian fashions with new materials according to contemporary concepts of comfort, mobility, and fabric care. Use antique Victorian apparel as guides for colors, cut, and ornamentation. (*See also Dancing, Fabrics, Fans, Underclothes, Weddings*)

Further Reading: Gernsheim, Alison. *Victorian and Edwardian Fashion* (Dover Publications, 1963).

This fashion plate from an 1869 issue of Le Bon Ton suggests that these well-upholstered flowers of Victorian womanhood were the humanized form of the popular Victorian cabbage rose being admired by the lady in blue.

Color: Exterior

Nothing has drawn the attention of the world to the Victorian Revival in North America more than the repainting of old and new Victorian buildings in cheerful polychromatic color schemes. Every major American paint manufacturer now markets a line of historic colors intended for owners of Victorian residential and commercial buildings who want to achieve a fresh exterior decoration in the authentic, boutique, or "painted lady" style.

While the Victorian color consciousness of Americans was being raised, their personal color convictions sank into a psychological disorder that I call "color anxiety." This chromatic ailment is not new. It can be traced to Andrew Jackson Downing's mid-nineteenth-century advocacy of semi-neutral, earth-tone colors on the body and darker colors on the trim of Italianate and Gothic Revival buildings.

Color anxiety didn't become a significant factor in the marketing of paint until the 1870s and 1880s. Prior to the birth of ready-mixed paint manufacturers like Sherwin-Williams in 1866, all American paint was made at the job site. To position themselves in the ready-mixed marketplace, companies like Sherwin-Williams published color cards and architectural books illustrated with innovative color schemes. A century later, this product literature supplied the documentation for a revival of Queen Anne color schemes.

Southernmost House, Key West, Florida, shows the consequences of inconsistent color placement due to confusion about the architectural logic of the detailing.

Color anxiety makes color more important than architecture. As a professional color and design consultant, I try to reverse this by discussing architecture and its ornamentation prior to colors and their placements. Many people who contact me are in a gray funk, listing their color preferences as two or three shades of neutral gray. Therapy simply consists of forcing them to put a positive color adjective before "gray" or color noun after "grayish"—as in "reddish gray" or "grayish blue." Then darker and contrasting trim and accent colors can be selected.

As a general rule it is best to use a light, semi-neutral color on the body and paint the trim with darker colors, some areas of which

can be accented with brighter contrasting colors. Medium or dark body colors tend to overwhelm buildings and underplay the architectural effect. They also limit color choices for trim to much lighter colors, which tend to trivialize architectural ornament, especially when accented by bright colors. Rare indeed is the individual with color courage who follows a medium or dark body color to its logical conclusion with contrasting trim colors of equal value.

White intensified the primary color contrast of this blue-and-yellow Victorian home in San Francisco.

Owners of masonry houses sometimes feel compelled to abandon their personal but artificial color preferences in deference to the natural colors of brick or stone. This reverence for natural materials was advocated by the Late Victorians, Edwardians, and Arts and Crafts Movement, yet need not apply today. Rich trimming colors in green, brown, red, or grayed blue can do much to enliven a house in any color brick. Similarly, any color darkened to a near black and applied to the cornice crown moldings and gutters will lessen the effect of an ugly roof color.

Color: Interior

Coloring interior walls is more complex than coloring exterior walls. Interior walls are rarely treated as solid areas of color. Richly patterned and colored three-dimensional objects are commonly placed in front of them.

David Ramsay Hay, the famous Victorian "Decorative Painter to the Queen" from Edinburgh, believed colors could convey feelings but should not be used to copy natural effects. Hay said, "The tone is generally fixed by the choice of the furniture" and its upholstery. It was, in Hay's estimation, the thankless but heroic task of the decorative painter to harmonize the background colors of the walls with the colors of the existing foreground furnishings.

Citing specific colors for various Victorian rooms during different decades is a hopeless and confusing task. It is more useful to cite Hay's general prescriptions for Victorian rooms, which appeared in his popular 1828 *Laws of Harmonious Coloring,* reprinted in 1867 from the sixth London edition in Philadelphia as *The Interior Decorator.* He wrote that drawing rooms should convey "vivacity, gayety, and light cheerfulness with tints of brilliant colors." Dining rooms were best filled with "warm, rich, substantial" colors with few contrasts. Breakfast parlors benefited from colors "medial between drawing-room and dining room." However, the tone of libraries should be "rich and grave" imitating "the richness produced by the bookbinder's art." By contrast, bedrooms were best painted "light, cleanly, and cheerful" with more contrast between room and furniture than in any other room because "bed and window-curtains form a sufficient mass to balance a tint of equal intensity upon the walls." Hays felt that staircases, lobbies, and vestibules should be "cool, simple, and free of contrast" to achieve "architectural grandeur" and improve "the effects of the apartments which enter from them."

Hay was sensitive to the natural light that rooms receive, something he called its "aspect." He said that rooms of summer residences lit from the south and west "should be cool in their coloring." Those from the north and east "ought to approach a warm tone," likewise for all the "apartments of a town house." He was also sensitive to Victorian artificial lighting. "All are of a warm or yellow tone. All cool colors are injured by the effects of such lights, while warm colors, from their being allied to red, are improved in brilliancy."

Interior decoration is not a democracy. Nor should it be chaos or tyranny. At its best, it is a genteel republic or enlightened monarchy. Something—a color or pattern or style—has to be given the lead, and everything else plays supporting roles. The most sucessful Victorian Revival rooms are apt to be those identifiable by Hay's romantic descriptions, in which a balance of colors is essential.

Honolulu House in Marshall, Michigan, is a splendid example of Victorian interior color design.

Dancing

By today's standards, all forms of Victorian ballroom dancing appear sedate, genteel, and innocent. According to Victorian ideals, some dances were criticized as dangerous, indecent, and intoxicating. When you consider the jerking and bouncing of the polka in quick 2/4 time, it's easy to imagine prim Victorians resisting its popularity beginning in the 1840s. But when proper Victorians protested the nineteenth century's most popular dance—the waltz—it's beyond our comprehension.

A Nervous Splendor, Frederic Morton's spell-binding 1979 book about Vienna 1888/1889, mentions "the wild and giddy Viennese waltz that had superseded the reasoned measures of the minuet." Johann Strauss—The Waltz King from the 1860s until his death in 1899—"was [in 1888] the world's first pop celebrity second only to Queen Victoria in international popularity polls." Morton quotes a Victorian critic who called the Viennese waltz "African and hot-blooded, crazy with life."

Victorian forms of social dancing continued to be popular until World War I, as seen in this 1913 Parisian illustration of the Lancer's Quadrille.

Although ballroom dancing ceased being chic in America during the 1960s, it recently has experienced a resurgence—as much for its exercise value as for its elegant, romantic associations. A Victorian

This newspaper illustration captures the "wild and giddy Viennese waltz . . . African and hot blooded, crazy with life."

Revival ball in period costume is an immensely appealing concept, but practical matters must be considered before you get committed.

Researching and making ball gowns could be a delightful activity, but are all the women willing to exercise strenuously in them for several hours? If a woman dressed in contemporary clothing occupies four square feet of space when dancing, a woman in Victorian costume will occupy nine to sixteen square feet—and may have trouble sitting down in such an outfit.

It would be more effective and profitable to stage a gala by renting costumes for a small company of professional ballroom dancers and having them competently perform some or all of the popular Victorian dances: polka, waltz, galop, lancers, polonaise, mazurka, schottische, and Highland schottishe. If you want to explore the pleasures of these dances for their own sake, then do so without the encumbrances of Victorian ballroom apparel.

Dining Room

Possessing a room dedicated to formal dining was not a dream exclusive to the Victorians—it was an old goal and remains so. Victorians who "took lodgings" had to fight for food on a daily basis in a common dining area with the famous "boarding-house reach." Those "in service" ate in common in the servant's hall or kitchen. Those at the lowest levels of home ownership fed themselves in multi-purpose rooms. Victorian dining rooms divided those who ate from those who dined.

In the sexist scheme of Victorian interior decoration, the dining room was commonly given a male atmosphere, with dark and som-

Late Victorian dining rooms in any mansion style tend to look like board rooms, especially when they are stripped of their dining accoutrements. This expressed the Victorian adage that "a man's castle was his home," or his throne-room, hence the throne-like armchair for him at "the head of the table."

ber colors, ample proportions, heavy furniture, and ornamentation featuring animals of the hunt. The theme was man as provider and hunter even though all most incumbents did was bring home the bacon on a regular basis. Unless you inherited or bought such items at a good price, there is no reason why you have to perpetuate this Victorian ideology in your own dining room.

This middle-class dining room is a more accessible model for today's Victorian lovers. Note the lambrequin on the clock shelf.

You can have a Victorian dining room without an authentic Victorian dining table. When fully arrayed, Victorian dining tables were completely covered with tablecloths. If your dining table fails to strike the right historic note, hide it with your finest linens and deck it out with formal table settings. That puts a dazzling collection of artifacts at the center of the room's natural focal point, and the white linen will brighten the room and intensify the positive colors seen against it.

If your dining table is gorgeous, the temptation is great to display it instead of the table settings and food, thereby upsetting the proper order of things. The function of any dining room is the presence of food that looks good and the consumption of food that tastes good. Everything else in the room is stagecraft for that event.

Down-scaled dining areas in today's tract houses have no room for over-scaled Victorian sideboards. They are also obsolete. Since most dining rooms lack servants and only service two-course meals consisting of a platter with salad and dessert, a sideboard is neither required for the carving of meats nor the delivery and removal of great quantities of crockery and cutlery. With so few takers, sideboards are readily available and they are inexpensive compared to dining tables and china cabinets. If you find one you like at an affordable price and space is available, install it with pride, for it can be a handsome decorative addition as well as handy on those holiday occasions when more formal dining takes place.

Don't despair your lack of a sideboard. The name reveals that it was originally nothing more than a board supported on trestles at the side of the table; then it evolved into a decorative casepiece. Any side table can function as a handsome sideboard when it is draped with linen.

The wonderful use of white lace on the table and windows is compromised by the white ceiling, which draws the eye up when it should be focused down on the altar of hospitality. The bay window has been cleverly converted from a mini-conservatory to an auxiliary dining center, possibly for the children of family and guests. This photograph shows that dining rooms need table furnishings, flowers, food, and people—especially people—to bring them to life.

Another object that people feel they must have in their dining room is a chandelier. Unless you inherit one, don't bother to get one. The dining room will be visually and functionally improved by its absence. A lead crystal chandelier diverts attention from the dining table and detracts from the spaciousness of the room. Overhead lighting is less flattering and romantic than candles on the table fired up for formal dining. Additionally, candle smoke deposits soot on the chandelier, which requires major effort to remove.

Floor covering is a personal option governed by economics, practicality, and general expectations. Before you make a major investment in an expensive textile for the floor, contemplate worst-case scenarios. Spilled red wine, for example, is devastating to rugs. Your guests didn't come to stand and look at your floor, so don't become obsessive about the appearance. The best floor covering would be a modern stain-resistant one with a solid-color center. It should be at least as large as your dining table when extended. The carpet might also have a border with a colorful but not too insistent pattern in harmony with the general decorative scheme.

Any tableware in a traditional style is acceptable in a Victorian dining room. The plates don't have to be porcelain, nor must the glasses be crystal. The cutlery doesn't have to be solid silver or plated. The only non-negotiable appointment is the linens. (*See also Chairs, Etiquette, Floral Decoration, Linens, Rugs and Carpets, Silverware*)

Dogs, Cats, and Other Pets in Art

Lap dogs were an appendage of eighteenth-century French ladies. Hunting dogs were a fixture of eighteenth-century British squires. But no people went to the dogs so completely as Victorians, who sentimentalized them in many forms of art. Too much has been made of the influence Victoria and Albert had on every conceivable aspect of Victorian life. However, this is one instance where they can be held directly responsible through their patronage of the artist Edwin Landseer, who had been specializing in paintings of dogs

Sir Edwin Landseer, "A Scene at Abbotsford."

and animals for more than twenty years before Victoria's coronation in 1837. Francis Lichten's *Decorative Art of Victoria's Era* (1950), refers to Landseer as the "petted darling of English fashion. He not only was the Royal Family's favorite painter, but also was ranked as the greatest artist of the English-speaking world."

Landseer was an accomplished technician, but his world-wide reputation promoted by engravings of his most popular works depended more on the sentimentality of his subject matter than the artistic brilliance of his paintings. Landseer's most beautiful dog portrait was his 1842 "Eos"—one of Prince Albert's graceful greyhounds. A model of the dog cast in zinc was a highlight of the 1851 Crystal Palace Exhibition. Afterward, it was pirated by an American cast-iron manufacturer and sold as a popular Victorian lawn ornament or metal guard dog for the gates or entrances of Victorian homes.

With the double-barrel approval of art and royalty, Victorian popular arts—especially those of packaging and advertising—made unlimited use of sentimental pictures of dogs, cats, and other pets. Publishers of colored engravings and lithographs offered pet series. Popular pottery used them. It was a period in which cats and dogs reigned in the decorative arts.

Sir Edwin Landseer, "Alexander and Diogenes."

Doors

"Pocket" doors that would slide into wall cavities was an old technique for hiding doors, but Late Victorian designers tried to eliminate doors completely by replacing them with heavy drapes called "portieres." E.C. Gardner's *Home Interiors* (1878) said a swinging door took up 30 or 40 square feet (3 or 4.2 sq m) of a wall space and from 15 to 20 square feet (1.6 to 2 sq m) of a floor. If they couldn't be gotten rid of, they were transformed into a collection of framed artwork panels decorated with pictures of plants and animals. The same thing was done with etched glass panels of exterior doors.

Despite a healthy market for reproduction Victorian doors, few look authentic. They are often expensive, over-wrought collections of beveled-edge and engraved plate glass in hardwood frames costing several thousands of dollars, especially when purchased with neoclassical sidelights and transoms. Despite the immense variety of surviving Victorian doors that could be copied by contemporary manufacturers, most Victorian Revival doors differ only in the amount and patterning of expensive plate glass pieces. Until the typical Victorian Revival door stops looking like a casino entrance, builders of serious Victorian Revival buildings will have to make do with architectural salvage.

Deciding how to finish a Victorian door depends upon the state of the wood. If it is in good condition and merits presentation for its own sake, give it a natural finish. If not, you can stain and finish, woodgrain, or paint it to look like your favorite wood. You could paint it the darkest trim color or a greenish black. (*See also Entrances, Portieres*)

Faceted glass in the entrance, arranged by lead cames into elaborate patterns reminiscent of Elizabethan knot-garden designs, make this Mid-Victorian hallway magical. The panel in the door and its sidelights may be of a later period than the cranberry-colored flashed glass cut-to-clear in the transom.

Dormers

The word dormer, by its connections with the French verb *dormir,* to sleep, and the Latin *dormitorium,* a place to sleep, originally meant a bedroom window. Since the French tended to locate the bedrooms of their children and servants in the attic, the term came to signify a window in the roof.

One of the major goals of Victorian architectural design was a building with lively rooflines. Dormers were the most important architectural detail used to break up and enliven monotonous roof areas. Architects also used balconies, turrets, towers, multicolored slates and shingles, ornate cornices, finials, bargeboards, and crestings, but all of them could be eliminated and the roof remain interesting as long as it had dormers.

Since the recent perfection of reliable, efficient, and economically installed skylights, dormers have been increasingly regarded as an obsolete technology for admitting light and air. This may be compelling for contemporary architects seeking undisturbed and uncluttered roof slopes, but Victorian architects sought more complexity in their designs.

This Austin, Texas, home displays an elaborate dormer.

Dovecotes and Other Birdhouses

Bird cages for canaries, a favorite Victorian pet, were common in middle-class Victorian homes. The cages hung outdoors during pleasant weather. Victorian cottages often had homemade, permanent birdhouses in their yards. Although they had simple details, they were made in every fashionable style of Victorian domestic architecture. Why should "our feathered friends" be domiciled any differently than ourselves, was the line of reasoning.

Woodward's Architectural and Rural Art for 1867 had a design for a side-gabled birdhouse with deep eaves, side piazzas, and a front Mansardic tower with second-floor balcony. A combination box-pillared take-up reel for a clothesline and hipped-roof birdhouse appeared in an 1884 book called *Household Conveniences.* Although clothes dryers have made washlines obsolete for most people, a pair of these might be installed on a tennis court to mask the steel posts and provide storage for equipment.

Another type of birdhouse was the pigeon house, or dovecote. A design for a "City Barn" that appeared in George Barber's *Cottage Souvenir, No. 2* of 1891 shows the entire side gable fitted out with a dovecote. It had arched niches reminiscent of an Ancient Roman architectural feature called a columbarium, which is another name for pigeon house.

This miniature octagon house is almost too good for the common birds of the air.

Eclecticism

For some people, the term eclectic connotes a haphazard and mediocre assortment of objects. This is far from the case, however, for those who wish to take this approach to decorating their Victorian Revival home. It's time to restore eclectic to its proper dictionary definition of "choosing what appears to be the best from diverse sources, systems, or styles."

Many eclectic Victorian designs are abysmal failures—some so bad they are comically delightful. But many more combined details taken from the arts of various times and places in such a way that each detail was given new life in a new time and a new place.

Victorians had a reverence for history, but few felt bound by the dogmatic need to slavishly copy the artistic monuments of different cultures. Despite their devotion to the arts of the past, most Victorians prided themselves on being "of today." Victorians believed that modern times should be characterized by a democratic kind of eclectic art, in which all styles were good fellows. They kept an open mind toward all vintage and exotic designs and considered the potential of each to contribute to a new international style. The Victorians felt that such a new style might rival the importance and longevity of the Ancient Greek and Roman achievements.

This spectacular room demonstrates the contemporary comprehension of "typically Victorian" interior decoration in terms of its eclecticism, clutter, and romanticism. Note the variety of Early Victorian lighting devices and Mid-Victorian furniture. The collection of porcelain-headed dolls is impressive, but also note the Victorian dog art on the walls, the painting on glass over the bedstead, and the needlepoint rugs. The wallpaper is an overscaled version of a paisley shawl.

Entertainments

Victorians were never at a loss for entertainment and invented countless charming ways to divert themselves. Pleasures were relished more thoroughly simply because most Victorians were in less of a hurry than we are today and had to rely more on their own imaginations to keep themselves amused.

Despite the opulent offerings of video entertainments, favorite events for most families today remain Victorian ones: holiday gatherings, birthdays and anniversaries, family reunions, picnics, horse races, boating, bicycling, hot-air ballooning, skating, political clambakes, parades, amateur theater, outdoor concerts, touring, visiting seaside or mountain resorts, and strolling around the neighborhood.

The circus as we know it today was also a Victorian entertainment. Phineas Taylor Barnum opened his "Greatest Show on Earth" in 1871 and merged with his biggest competitor to form Barnum and Bailey in 1881.

There are many at-home Victorian entertainments that deserve to be revived. It seems pointless to perpetuate the sexism of a Victorian tea party, so make it appealing to men as well as women with the substantial fare of a Victorian high tea. Pantomime is a Victorian tradition in Britain, especially around Christmas, but its techniques can be learned and used any time of the year. The Victorian dessert party is another delightful social occasion and is an especially appropriate summertime event. It has the glamour of a dinner party without most of the bother. *Tableaux vivants*—famous pictures brought to life by costumed people—were favored by the Victorian gentry because they showcased beauty, fashion, and wit. If you and your friends enjoy the drama of dressing up and showing off but fear speaking parts, *tableaux vivants* are for you.

THE WORLD'S GREAT CIRCUS.
THE MARCH PAST.

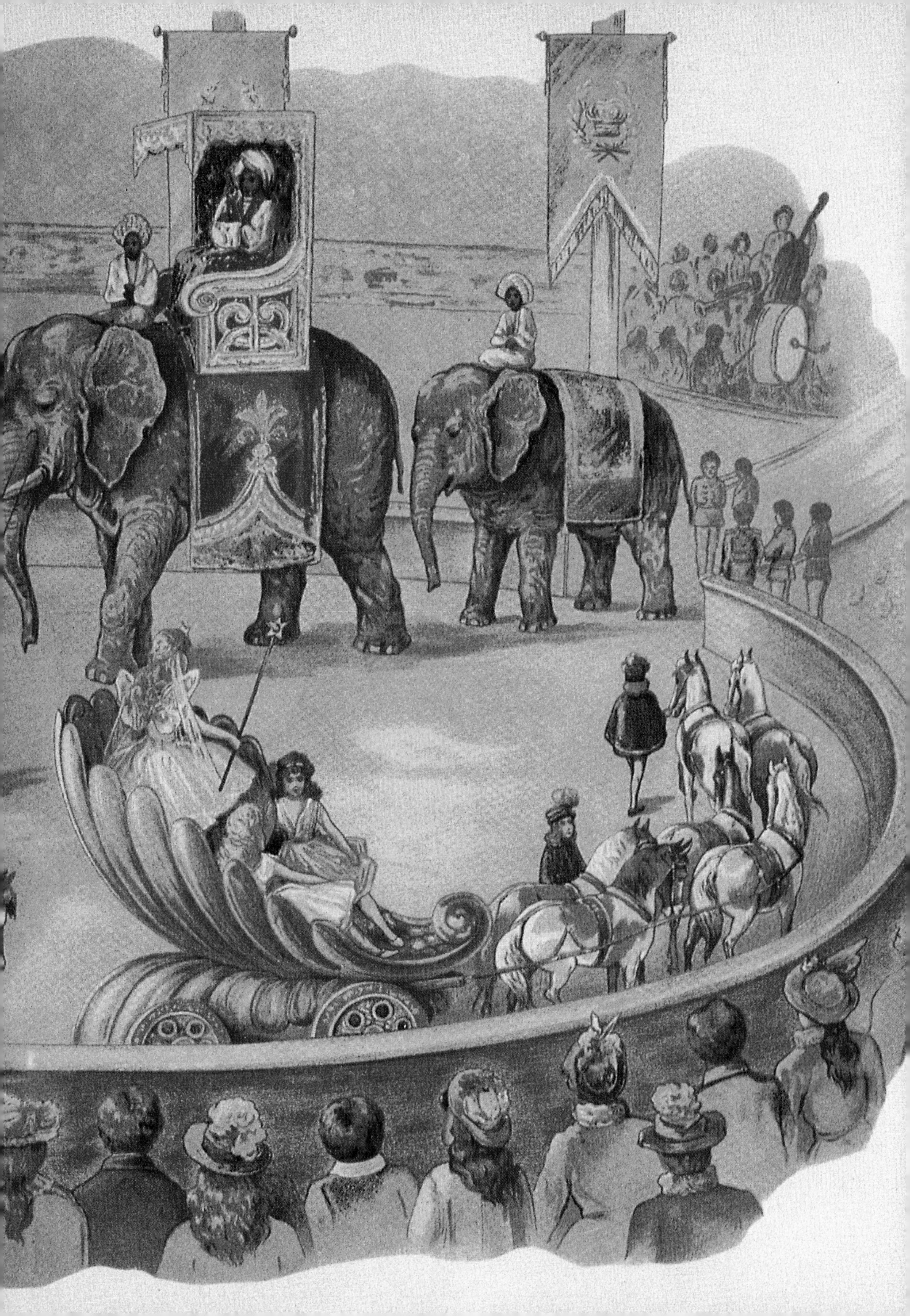

Entrances

Victorian architects appreciated the importance of making entrances, and they focused their ornamental flair on them more than any other building feature. Entrances are more than doors—they are gateways to different worlds. They are meant to convey a message about the home's inhabitants or the building's function. When you get an invitation to a formal dinner, you don't go to the kitchen door, you pass through the front entrance, leaving your personal behavior outside and obediently adopting the house rules of your host. This is the essence of etiquette.

The raised first floor of the Late Victorian Starret House in Port Townsend, Washington, is entered via a stoop with a porch on top.

Victorian home entrances frequently featured fancy casings, rich materials, colored and cut glass in the sashes, carved columns and panels, gilt detailing, sidelights and transoms. Many had canopies, balconies, and towers, but the most common feature was the porch.

Victorian architects placed porches perpendicular to entrances, but if the house had a verandah—a feature placed parallel to the walls of a house—they would position an entrance porch at right angles to the verandah. The primary function of porches was to give entrances a monumental quality.

The vestibule is a subsidiary component of Victorian entrances that merits revival for practical as well as social purposes. Interposed between the entrance door and the hall or living room, the vestibule functions as an air trap, keeping heated air in during the winter and cooled air in during the summer. Socially, the vestibule allows the entrance to be opened to strangers without letting them inside the house.

Victorians preferred architecture having zones of increasing social status. The visitor approached the house, walked to the verandah, passed through the formal entrance, stood in the holding area of a vestibule or hall, and was finally admitted into the formal parlor. If the visitor was an especially welcome guest, the social call might culminate in the ultimate reward any Victorian family could bestow—an invitation to the dining room. (*See also Verandahs and Porches*)

Étagère

This is the fancy French word for the infamous Victorian whatnot—actually a set of shelves meant to display knickknacks. Because it resembled a stack of open stages, it was appropriate to name it with the French word for "stage," especially when it was populated by a mini-museum of curiosities and souvenirs.

Along with wax fruit and flowers encased in a glass dome, the parlor center table, and the antimacassar—a protective doily attached to the backs of upholstered chairs and sofas to absorb macassar hair oil—the étagère is one of the enduring symbols of the Victorian period. It came in many forms: a straight-sided, tiered cake supported at the corners by turned posts; a flat-backed structure with a range of receding shelves; or an elaborately designed cabinet made from rare woods. The most popular form was supported by two triangular, fret-sawn boards joined together so the piece could fit into the corner of a room.

If you were a child at the time, the contents of a parlor étagère were bewitching. The writer Francis Litchen was ordinarily severe in her criticisms of Victorian decorative arts, but she had fond memories of her parent's whatnot. The following appeared in her *Decorative Art of Victoria's Era* (1950): "Indelibly engraved in the author's memory are the color and markings of a cross-section of petrified wood from Arizona's great forest, the heft and texture of a bit of dried star-fish, the pleasant smoothness of Japanese carved ivory—impressions imparted early in life by means of the trivia on a whatnot, of which not a bit of the original vividness has been lost."

The Aesthetic Movement, promoted in America by books like Clarence Cook's The House Beautiful (1878), influenced the acquisition and use of antiques, especially exotic antiques like this Chinese étagère. For those of the proper aesthetic mentality this was, in Cook's words, "an ornamental upholder of the monumental." Put to improper use by lesser sensibilities, it was the vehicle for the eclectic clutter that characterized the end of the nineteenth century and was so justly reviled in the early twentieth century.

ETIQUETTE

Victorians published more books about etiquette than any other people in history. They inherited a rich tradition of behavior books, foremost among them Henry Peacham's *The Compleat Gentleman*

FIG. 12. GENTILITY IN THE DINING-ROOM.

The evidences of good breeding with a party of ladies and gentlemen seated about a table, who are accustomed to the usages of polite society, are many. Among these will be the fact that the table is very beautifully and artistically spread. This need not require much wealth, but good taste is necessary to set it handsomely.

Again, the company evince gentility by each assuming a genteel position while eating. It is not necessary that an elaborate toilet be worn at the table, but careful attention should always be given to neatness of personal appearance, however plain may be the dress which is worn.

Another evidence of good manners is the self-possession with which the company deport themselves throughout the meal.

Good form versus bad form, as seen by Hill's Manual of Social and Business Forms, first published in 1870. Note that the monied partake "in the dining room"; the impoverished eat "at the table."

(1622). Victorians addressed the issue of hypocrisy and the social facade, cast into high relief by Lord Chesterfield's famous *Letters to His Son,* first published in 1774. Translated into Japanese in 1990 it became a best-seller in Japan as a guide to Western manners! In the West it is chiefly remembered as the target of eighteenth-century critic Samuel Johnson's famous barb that it was a system of advice promoting "the manners of a dancing master and the morals of a whore."

Victorian etiquette authors set themselves to the task of culling this material and adjusting the sophisticated ethics of eighteenth-century aristocratic behavior to nineteenth-century middle-class morality. This echoed Queen Victoria's efforts to give British monarchy bourgeois respectability.

Twentieth-century readers of Victorian etiquette books tend to study them as a collection of sectarian bibles serving the Victorian religion of Domesticity. Actually, they were a popular form of literature that Victorians read selectively for entertainment as well as information. The same could be said about twentieth-century etiquette books. Do you know anyone who has read Emily Post or Miss Manners cover-to-cover? Or followed their directions to the letter?

Most of the books were out of date when first published, popular ones more so with each reprinting. If you study them for time-specific information, much of what they say will have to be discounted by a factor of twenty years or more. For etiquette à la mode, read the newspapers and magazines of the period.

The ultimate proving ground of Victorian etiquette was the dining room. The best example of the difference in setting and manners between those who dine and those who eat appears in Thomas Hill's 1873 *Manual of Social and Business Forms.*

"Gentility in the Dining-Room" takes place in a formal setting. Windows have drapes and swagged lambrequins. There is gas lighting, a table cloth, and plush-bottomed seating. Everyone dresses for dinner, and a multiple-course meal is served by hired help. Art on the walls, a carpeted floor, and central heating enhance the atmosphere.

"Bad Manners at the Table" takes place in a multi-purpose room without windows. Vulgar kerosene lighting reveals an uncovered table and plank bottom seating. Everyday clothing is worn for dinner. It is a single-course meal without servants. A coat rack and crockery shelf on the wall, bare floor, and a stove in the room are other common details.

Fabrics

Weave, color, and current fashion were important factors in selecting fabrics in Victorian times. Victorians were sensitive to the difference between old-fashioned, vulgar cotton calico and fashionable, elegant cotton chintz.

Silk was the most elegant Victorian fiber and was prized—then as now—for its lightweight yet strong continuous thread and phenomenal affinity for dyes. The allure and profit potential of silk was so great that Americans throughout the Victorian period tried and failed to grow mulberry trees in North America capable of feeding silkworms. If silk fabric were divided along standard Victorian class lines expressed in terms of architecture, cottage silk was plain woven taffeta, villa silk was lustrous satin, and mansion silk was elaborate jacquard-loomed damask or brocade and dense-pile velvet or plush. Special-effect silks were water-marked moiré and metal-thread lamé.

Cotton benefited more than any other fiber from late eighteenth- and nineteenth-century developments in preparing, spinning, and looming. More specialized fabrics were developed from cotton than silk, linen, and wool combined. The most famous are gingham, calico, grosgrain, dimity, cambric, muslin, huckaback, ticking, lawn, crash, denim, dotted Swiss, repp, chintz, organdy, satin, brocade, and brocatelle. Victorian homes used cotton canvas for awnings and glazed cotton called holland cloth for roller shades.

Production of Victorian woolens and worsteds was improved by technical spinoffs from the cotton industry, but there were few innovations in wool felt and cloth. In contrast, linen production was devastated by the mass-production of cotton fabrics. Linen survived as the generic name for tablecloths and napkins because it was superior to cotton. It was stronger, smoother, more lustrous, more difficult to soil, and more resistant to absorbing and retaining moisture. The finest bleached, starched, and ironed linen is synonymous with purity, polish, and smoothness. Because linen thread is strong, it was used for fine lace. Because linen cloth feels cool, it was used for summer sheeting and summer clothing.

The linen name also survived in crinoline—an old textile combining horsehair and linen used to stiffen seventeenth-century farthingales and eighteenth-century whalebone-hoop petticoats. Victorian ladies at mid-century abandoned the old-fashioned hair-and-linen textile and multiple petticoats for a single, metal-hooped petticoat but retained the old name. The new device was instantly popular because it was light, had the profile of an open fan, which created the illusion of small waists without resort to tight corseting, and swayed alluringly to reveal seductive glimpses of ankles. Hence that part of the Victorian period is often called "The Crinoline Era."

Although horsehair disappeared from the Victorian crinoline, it was the basis of the period's most notorious fabric—black horsehair upholstery. It was and is still available in colors and woven patterns, but today's custom-made output is very expensive.

Despite the great innovations in Victorian spinning and weaving, they were trivial compared to the accidental discovery in 1856—the same year the metal-hoop crinoline was invented—of the first aniline dye by a teenage chemist named William Henry Perkin. The color he devised was first called Perkin's Violet. With disregard for accurate color names characteristic of the dye industry ever since, it was renamed mauve from the French cognate for the mallow flower. Magenta, a name for aniline fuschia that honored an 1859 battlefield victory by Napoleon III, made less sense than mauve. Both were sensational in silk gowns, especially when seen under harsh Victorian gaslights. The aniline dye industry, centered in Germany, created a succession of garish colors that revolutionized Victorian color sensibilities.

Fancy Work

Other terms for fancy work were adornments, ornaments, embellishments, and enrichments, often prefixed with the period's favorite word—elegant. It included decorative needlework but generally referred to a variety of popular art activities learned from books. Its practitioners used special kits of art materials to create small-scale home decorations. Today it's a major industry called "arts and crafts," or simply "crafts."

Victorian fancy-work guides were seductively grounded in the same treacherous assumption of today's craft guides: *You can do it!* Readers were promised they could learn rudimentary skills in drawing and color from a few paragraphs and a bit of practice. Ultimate Victorian fancy work reproduced fine art paintings and drawings.

Grecian painting was a method by which uncolored engravings and lithographs were converted into framed and colored imitation paintings. Prints were attached to a frame and rendered transparent by a coating of varnish on the back. After colors applied to the back

Victorian table cover.

were absorbed, the front was varnished and the paper mounted on canvas. J.E. Tilton published lithographs in Boston "expressly for Grecian painting," as well as *Art Recreations*—an 1859 book with color directions for painting their prints of *The Happy Family, Hiawatha's Wooing,* Darley's *The Marriage of John Alden,* and Correggio's *Madonna Della Scala,* among other works.

Decorated faïence by John Bennett, a gifted artist who worked for Doulton in Great Britain and moved to New York City, as illustrated in the inexactly titled Women's Handiwork in Modern Homes (1881)—an influential guidebook for the American Aesthetic Movement.

Oriental painting is better known today as painting-on-glass. It used sign-painting skills to make gaudy pictures of birds and flowers heightened with tinsel in the back against a black background. Tilton provided boxes of colors and outline drawings placed under the glass to guide the hand, including a design for the top of a chess table. Ground glass vases, lamp shades, and door panels were decorated with Oriental paintings minus the tinsel and black backgrounds.

Photographic painting was common prior to the twentieth-century invention of color film, but its original intent was imitating miniature portrait paintings. Tilton's *Art Recreations* criticized the ordinary portrait photograph as crowded "with gaudy bed-furniture curtains, old-fashioned chairs, vases of artificial flowers, plaster of Paris pillars, and the usual table placed so conveniently for the sitter to lean on [for the required long exposure]—making the head a secondary object." The photograph was given a coating of glue size before watercolors were applied.

Theorem painting used stencils to create designs, hence it was "better adapted to fruits, birds, and butterflies, than to landscapes and heads," said *Art Recreations.* Theorems were used on glass to make Oriental paintings as well as on wood and papier mâché, but its locus classicus was framed velvet. Dresses in silk, satin, or crepe were also decorated by theorem painting.

Less highbrow fancy work involved transferring preprinted images in color to glass, pottery, or porcelain variously called potichomanie, decalcomanie, diaphanie, and vitremanie. Transfers to window panes imitated stained glass. Oriental and European porcelains were imitated by using embroidery scissors to carefully cut out pictures, which were then transferred to the insides of glass vases.

After a coating of varnish was applied, the interior of the vase was swirled with paint that was "greenish white, bluish white, slight rose white, pale yellow, or pine color slightly brown," according to *Art Recreations.*

Those with sculptural skills tried their hands at casting and coloring wax fruit or modeling wax flowers, many examples of which survive. Leather work, something that *Art Recreations* proclaimed "when well and tastefully done, closely resembles rich carving in wood," has not survived well; dried and varnished, it eventually crumbled to dust. (*See also Berlin Work and Samplers, Ceramics, Floral Decoration, Linens, Lettering, Monograms, Needlework, Papier Mâché, Rustic Adornments, Roller Shades, Stenciling, Screens*)

"Portrait Plaque" hand-painted by Rosina Emmet, illustrated in Women's Handiwork in Modern Times (1881).

Fans

Victorians had two systems of personal air-conditioning—fans and "pray-for-breeze." One-piece fans and folding fans are ancient devices. The best ones were made of ivory and highly decorated with carvings, inlays, and paintings. The most extravagant fans were made in eighteenth-century France after which the art declined along with the aristocratic society it symbolized. French associations survived in the mechanized and vulgarized Victorian versions of fans.

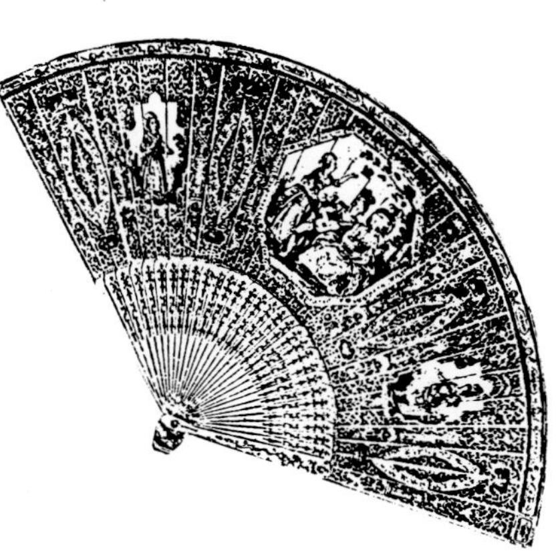

The fan also had its own symbolic language. When properly manipulated by a Victorian maiden, it was an amusing flirtatious device. Dramatically timed openings and closings, along with coy glances over the top, kept many Victorian entertainments rolling along nicely.

Late Victorians used oriental fans as colorful decorative accents in Aesthetic Movement interiors. Such fans were never framed, just opened and distributed with artful casualness on mantels, side-boards, plate rails, etc. to satisfy—along with an equally aesthetic assortment of oriental prints and porcelain—the obligatory note of japonism. (*See also Japonism*)

For a Victorian lady a fan was as essential as a hanky, as shown in an 1869 issue of Le Bon Ton.

FENCES

An attractive fence positions a Victorian house in its landscape. This one belongs to a Gothic Revival house with Italianate detailing in Old Lyme, Connecticut.

Victorian fences are like Victorian verandahs. They deteriorate rapidly with neglect, are soon removed, and are rarely restored. This is unfortunate, because the exterior decoration of a Victorian home can be enriched at modest expense by a well-built, sensitively colored, and regularly maintained fence.

Fences are not exercises in hand and foot railings. They are more symbolic than utilitarian and are made more visually interesting by balusters, finials, and posts. It's best to use standard railings from your local building supply. If your fence integrates railings into the caps and bases of the posts, standard railings can be rip-sawn and mortised for the purpose.

Cut the profiles of the balusters with a bandsaw one at a time or in bundles. You can make the cut-outs inside the balusters with a saber saw or jigsaw, but that takes time, weakens the balusters, and creates points that eventually fill with paint. Victorians didn't do it, but it's more practical to stencil the cut-out patterns with paint having a value or color that contrasts with the baluster.

You can copy the colors of your house or verandah in your fence. But it's more effective to color your fence in contrast to your house, your landscape, and street plantings. Railings integrated with posts can have two colors: one for posts/railings and one for balusters/finials. If railings are not integrated with posts and you want to make them and their balusters appear to horizontally pierce the verticals of the posts, you can have three colors: one for posts, one for balusters/finials, and one for railings.

Avoid any design with a V or X that channels water to a point where wood will rot. To minimize water damage, prime all planes of the fence components prior to assembly. Pressure-treated wood might be used for parts in direct contact with the ground. Otherwise use regular lumber and boards.

It's easier to paint all balusters and railing prior to final assembly. Paint to pencil lines indicating areas sunk into railings. After assembly, a few swipes with a paintbrush will seal the joints.

Floors

"What *shall* we do with our floors?" was a common Victorian lament. The problem was determining the fashionable relationship between floors and floor coverings, especially wall-to-wall floral carpets. For many Victorians, revealing the natural materials of their floors was a raw necessity instead of a conscious aesthetic goal before mid-century factories made carpeting affordable to the middle-class. Beginning in the 1860s, critics censured carpets as unsanitary and difficult to keep clean and ridiculed the nonsense of walking on counterfeit indoor flower gardens. They banished interior carpet bedding back to the lawn from whence it came and urged a return to the reality of wood floors.

Late Victorians substituted textile simulations of gardens with other forms of illusion for wood floors. Topping the list was elaborate wood mosaic called *parquetry.* E.C. Gardner's *Home Interiors* of 1878 described it as "a floor composed of wooden triangles and trapesiums laid by trick of form and color [to] make the floor appear like a lot of little cubes set corner-wise, a succession of troughs or miniature mountain-ranges." Gardner grumbled, "Such ought to be looked upon as practical jokes, not sober realities."

Ignoring his dictum about making floors appear "simple, natural, level, and smooth," many Late Victorians made their floors look like tiles, marbles, floor cloths, or parquetry—anything but plain wood. They did so by staining, graining, marbling, stenciling, and decorative painting—a group of art forms known today as *faux finishes.*

Throughout the Victorian period real tiles and marbles were used in fancier houses in high-traffic areas of vestibule and hallway as well as the damp areas of bathroom and conservatory. British encaustic tiles by Maw or Minton were favored for public rooms. Plain tiles of local or imported manufacture were used for kitchens and other utilitarian areas.

Naturally finished floors are fashionable now, but few things are less Victorian. If you respect Victorian floors, don't chemically

Alternating light and dark strips of wood create this boldly energized parquet floor. The crowded hanging of many gold-framed paintings with visible wires is appropriate for the period.

Simple, alternating squares in two sizes and two colors creates a regal entrance floor. The marbleized walls are examples of the grainers' art.

strip, scrape, or sand away Victorian colored varnish, colored stain, and colored filler and give it a clear and glossy finish. Ordinary Victorians finished common softwood flooring in their cottages and villas to imitate the fine hardwoods, parquety, marbles, or tiles in mansions. They would be mystified by contemporary floors finished to look freshly minted. The last thing any Victorian wanted was a floor that looked new. By all means, if you wish to attempt such an ambitious finish for your floor, do so. But do not feel you have to go to great lengths to decorate your floor. Since a sparsely-furnished Victorian room is a contradiction in terms, a major portion of the floor will be concealed. Decorate the floor last to harmonize with the decoration of the room. It takes less courage and ability to balance the scale, color, and character of a pattern on the floor with everything else in the room than vice versa.

Floral Decoration

Sentimentalism was the Victorian period's favorite brand of romanticism. Landseer and his imitators supplied so many sweet images of dogs and cats that some rooms looked more like pet palaces than homes for humans. (*See Dogs, Cats, and Other Pets in Art*) This was a Victorian trifle compared to sentimentalized floral decoration. "When in doubt, decorate with flowers," was the precept of Victorian interior decoration.

Among today's most popular leisure activities are flower gardening and arranging—a natural consequence of an enormous horticultural industry rooted in the Victorian period. However, few people look at flowers today and use them to decorate their interiors with Victorian intensity and sentimentality. Few have the leisure time of that hothouse Victorian variety of woman called "the accomplished lady."

Victorians rationalized floral decoration—real or fake, temporary or permanent—by the principle that the ideal state of being in this life was "Union Between Humanity and Nature." They did everything possible to connect the outdoor world to interiors and physically bring it indoors. Victorians placed verandahs, bay windows, balconies, towers, and cupolas to maximize the prospects of lawns and flower gardens in the foreground and distant fields, woods, waters, and hills. Before wire screening for windows came into general use in the 1870s, Victorians opened French doors and both parts of double-hung sash to maximize fresh-air ventilation.

If you can't put people dressed in Victorian fashions in your interiors, the next best thing is floral arrangements.

Mansions had controlled environment conservatories, which made nonstop indoor gardening with exotic tropical plants possible. Villas and cottages could do likewise, albeit on a much smaller scale. These homes had terrariums called Wardian cases after the man who invented the container used by nineteenth-century plant collectors to transport plants from exotic locations to Europe and the Eastern United States.

Victorians would envy the perfection of today's silk flowers. They had to be content with arrangements of natural flowers dried

Vick's Flower and Vegetable Garden *shows how to decorate a parlor with ivy.*

in sand or imitation flowers of wax, paper, leather, shells, or feathers, which they protected from dust under glass domes and placed on the ubiquitous parlor center table. Sheets of colored wax for making wax flowers are available today in most craft shops.

At a recent symposium of the Victorian Society in America, Ellen McClelland Lesser discussed the problems modern minds have comprehending the Victorian mentality of using live flowers for decoration. Today's arrangements are expected to endure for a week or more. Victorian ones were expected to survive only a few hours. According to Ms. Lesser, the nicest compliment any host could offer guests was personally creating a fresh flower arrangement from one's own garden, just for them and just for the moment of presentation. Ms. Lesser says the first step of learning the Victorian mode is the hardest. You have to forget what you were taught about modern arrangements, especially everything Japanese. Victorians liked massive arrangements of big flowers with rich colors densely packed in concentric circles. The look and feel of upholstery was the ideal: the more stuffed and ruffled, the better.

On a smaller scale, Victorians developed bouquet design into a decorative art. Bouquet makers selected their flowers according to a vocabulary of sentimentalized attributes. (*See Language of the Flowers*)

Source: Ellen McClelland Lesser provides consultation on Victorian floral arrangements. PO Box 151, Stuyvesant, NY 12173.

GABLES

Gables are architectural details of particularly Victorian sentiment. The most famous Victorian literary gables are the seventeenth-century New England *House of Seven Gables* by Hawthorne and the nineteenth-century Prince Edward Island *Anne of Green Gables* by Lucy Montgomery.

Because gables rise above and peek through surrounding foliage, they are natural locations for ornamentation of various kinds. Gables possess the ability to make the first and most lasting impressions. Often they are aided by peak ornaments, bargeboards, brackets, and other kinds of cornice drapery. Late Victorian gables often have overscaled windows. Sometimes they are penetrated by bay windows, balconies, or towers.

Today's best-known variety of Victorian gable is the one with decorative shingles, common to Late Victorian and Edwardian buildings. Fish-scale shingles are the most famous shape, but there were many other kinds—all of which imitated the decorative tiles of European vernacular buildings. One shape or several in combination might be used to create decorative bands. Whether one band or many, each appears to cry out for a special "accent" color.

This Peoria, Illinois, home sports a beautifully balanced gable.

Games

After dividing games from sports, Victorians separated games into four categories: those for children, adults, indoor parlors, and outdoor lawns. The best games were those in which both adults and children could participate. A few games, like croquet, were played both inside and outside. The indoor version was called parlor or tabletop croquet and was played with miniature equipment.

Victorian books of parlor games for both children and adults emphasized verbal games, especially those of a moralizing nature. One need only read them today to recapture the principle of the game, which can be given a more modern context. If any game strikes you as dull, it probably was likewise for the Victorians. Just because something was a game didn't mean it was fun. No amount of modernization can bring it to life. Move on to the next selection.

If you prefer card games, you might revive a Victorian game. Unless your group is composed of devoted historians of its favorite game, select one unknown to all. If you revive a Victorian version of your favorite game, you will only discover why it was discarded, and there is no fun in that.

Victorian board games are now a coveted collectible. It would be entertaining as well as educational to invite a local collector of Victorian board games to make a display and select some for play by your party.

"A Game of Flowers" is taken from At Home Again by S. G. Sowerby and Thomas Crane and published by Marcus Ward, one of the leading publishers for the British Aesthetic Movement. Thomas Crane was Walter Crane's brother.

Hats

Fashion enthusiasts of the late twentieth century are slowly cultivating an appreciation for the practicality, beauty, and symbolism of hats, but they are a long way from regaining Victorian passion for them. Work and leisure hats are popular today, but social hats are not as fashionable as they once were. As feminism matures, fear of skin cancer rises, and appreciation of the past is nurtured, it seems more than likely that in the next century there will be a hat revival.

Like other Victorian decorative objects, Victorian hats began as simple forms and evolved into more complex styles. The richest variety, predictably, was in women's hats. Fancy millinery, however, was an urban fashion. One of my Victorian ancestors discovered this the hard way when she took her city millinery skills, of which she was immensely proud, to a rural town and set up shop. Although the place was a county seat, her clientele didn't want fancy hats; they wanted plain bonnets. She nearly starved.

The prettiest Victorian woman's hat was the bonnet because of its ability to frame the face. The earliest Victorian bonnets almost buried a woman's head within when viewed from the side. Thus hidden or obscured, the impact of a woman's facial features when they came into full view was further intensified by a lined brim trimmed inside with flowers, which nearly encircled the face.

A popular Late Victorian summer hat for both men and women was a stiff-brimmed, oval straw hat called a "boater." The locus classicus of the boater is Cowes in the Isle of Wight, headquarters of the Royal Yacht squadron and where the regatta season culminates in Cowes week during the first week in August. It is also the location of Osborne, a county seat built in 1845 for Queen Victoria and Prince Albert. Of all her royal residences, Victoria preferred Osborne, and she died there in 1901.

The most famous Victorian hat is the black silk top hat. It was worn by men to official occasions and the most elegant affairs well into the twentieth century. The most famous Victorian top hat is Abraham Lincoln's stovepipe.

Fashionable hats for 1869 from Le Bon Ton (following page).

LE BON TON

Journal de Modes

Chapeaux de la M^{on} Leroy & Albert. Coiffeur de S. M. l'Impératrice r. St Honoré. 422.

Highland Style

Sir Walter Scott was the epitome of Victorian romanticism. Through his writings, which were enormously popular on both sides of the Atlantic, he tartanized Scottish history with such mastery that he captivated the imagination of Queen Victoria, who built her beloved Balmoral in the Scottish Highlands, and enthralled the world. He accomplished much more than improving the market for Scottish woolens and real estate; he created a general enthusiasm for medieval antiquities.

The first pilgrimage church of nineteenth-century British romanticism was Scott's home at Abbotsford, which had medieval architectural salvage details. It was decorated by David Ramsay Hay beginning in 1820. (*See also Color: Interior*) If the real thing couldn't be found, Scott had it made and "antiqued," thereby initiating one of the most characteristic—and reviled—of Victorian decorative techniques.

Abbotsford from the River Tweed.

Horses

One of the most enduring Victorian popular songs is Stephen Foster's *Camptown Races*. Many of the great traditions of the race course were established during the Victorian period. Winners of famous races were memorialized in paintings and lithographs.

Throughout the period horses remained important, giving it an aroma and character that can only be revived at today's horse shows. Yet, during the Late Victorian decades, steam railways and electric street cars made horses obsolete for major transport. At this time a new generation of Victorian gentry romanticized them and all of their paraphernalia into "The Country Life," of which the most recent version has been undertaken by Ralph Lauren, Inc.

A Currier and Ives.

INGLENOOK

An inglenook, strictly speaking, is a chimney corner, but Late Victorians and their successors in the early twentieth century applied it to any cozy spot behind the plane of a wall or under a staircase and shortened the term to "nook." For those who grew up in such places, inglenooks were the most romantic parts of the house. The built-in bench seating softened by loose cushions makes inglenooks look perfect for children. With stained-glass windows magically transforming daylight, a fireplace implying warmth, and a cushioned recess suggesting comfort, inglenooks were like a loving hug.

The restoration of the Turner House in West Newton, Massachusetts, features a Bradbury & Bradbury wallpaper frieze in the Peacock pattern.

IRONWORK

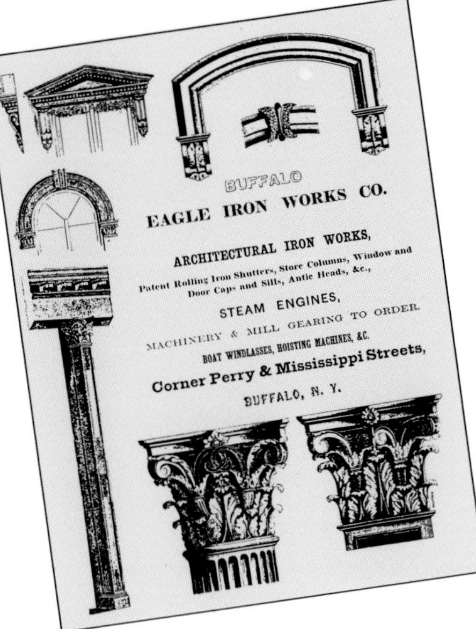

Iron had been in use for centuries prior to the nineteenth century, but Victorians were the last people to make major use of it. Victorians proudly called their century an Iron Age.

Only recently has there been an appreciation of Victorian decorative ironwork that escaped twentieth-century wars, wartime scrap drives, and postwar urban developments. Victorian wrought iron fared better during the twentieth century than ornamental cast iron because wrought iron was hand-made art and cast iron was factory-made artifice. Wrought iron went into museums or was recycled in new buildings because it had Gothic or Renaissance associations. Cast iron went into the scrap pile because it looked Victorian.

Victorian cast-iron buildings are now admired for the decorative qualities of their facades as well as the structural innovations of their framing. The cast-iron lace of Victorian verandahs is prized wherever it has survived. Cast-iron furniture, fencing, and architectural detailing is once again available.

The most delightful form of metal furniture is wire furniture, especially when it is used in a conservatory setting, as in the Glen Michaels residence in Troy, Michigan.

Islamic

The colors and patterns of Islamic pottery, tiles, and textiles were the height of exotic romanticism for Victorians attuned to such matters. Any serious practitioner of Victorian decorative arts was soon drawn to them. Rarely was the term Islamic used. What are now called oriental carpets, Victorians would have called Turkey carpets. Architecture, decoration, pottery, and tiles would have been called Moorish.

Turkey carpets, for those who could afford them, were as far as many Victorians went in decorating their homes with Islamic designs. Moorish appealed to Late Victorian artists like the masterful landscape painter Frederick Church, whose Olana overlooking the Hudson River is decorated outside and inside with Moorish colors, patterns, and artifacts. Louis Comfort Tiffany devoted a corner of his famous studio to a cozy melange of Moorish objects, some of his own design. Late Victorian homes with aesthetic pretensions sometimes daringly imitated the bohemian look of an artist's studio with what was called a Turkish Corner. Old photographs of them look like the disheveled aftermath of a drunken buying spree through an Algerian Casbah. Perhaps you had to be there to appreciate them properly.

Perhaps the best example of Islamic motifs in a surviving Victorian interior is the magical home of landscape painter Frederic Church at Olana, New York, overlooking the Hudson River. Note the brass peacocks flanking the fireplace. Note also the effective use of a decorated screen.

JAPONISM

Japanese ceramics enhance almost any interior, especially a Late Victorian one.

Commodore Perry's opening of Japan to trade with the West in 1853 exposed Victorian decorative arts to exotic and refreshing systems of Japanese design. International Exhibitions in London (1862) and Paris (1867) featured impressive collections of Japanese decorative arts, which stimulated the "chinamania" collecting of Japanese ceramics. But not until the Centennial Exhibition of 1876 in Philadelphia, when the West directly confronted living Japanese and their arts in a Japanese house and garden, did Japonism have a significant impact upon Victorian design.

A young generation of Victorian designers, depressed by what they perceived as dim prospects for further innovation within the Western decorative arts tradition, searched for univeral design principles and discovered in Japan the answers to their dreams. Christopher Dresser, Britain's leading design professor of the Aesthetic Movement, visited Japan after he attended the 1876 Centennial and wrote *Japan: Its Architecture, Art and Art Manufacturers,* which was published 1882 in London. Japan became the shortcut for any Victorian designer with an ounce of youth in his or her veins to create something new and different.

Whenever the adjectives art, artistic, or aesthetic were applied to objects during the 1870s and 1880s—as in *art furniture*—they were certain to be greatly influenced by Japanese design. Wallpaper, textiles, and other mediums that emphasized pattern were orientalized by Late Victorian designers.

JEWELRY

One of the most overlooked Victorian decorative arts is jewelry. Hairwork jewelry composed of human locks snipped from the hair of a corpse, Victorians regarded as a beautiful memento of the dearly departed, though the concept elicits shudders today. Jewelry made from an especially dense form of coal called jet is likewise regarded by many people today as vulgar.

Jet jewelry survives in quantity because it isn't good for anything else. Other Victorian jewelry that has endured to the present are cameos, enamels, and cloisonné. This is because they do not contain gems, and therefore are not worth disassembling for other purposes. Victorian jewelry containing valuable gems was usually dismantled and reset, and the metal was melted down—unless it was heirloom jewelry protected by its sentimental value.

Brooch in the Renaissance style by Carlo Giuliano, whose pieces are some of the most desirable of Victorian jewelry.

Kashmir Shawls

"Consider the beautiful Indian shawls and scarves and table-covers," wrote Christopher Dresser in his *Principles of Decorative Design* (1873). "Observe the manner in which small portions of intense reds, blues, yellows, greens, and a score of tertiary tints, are combined with white and black and gold to produce a very miracle of bloom."

Victorians inherited an intense admiration for them from the late eighteenth century. Francis Lichten's *Decorative Art of Victoria's Era* (1950) called the Kashmir shawl "the 'mink coat' of its period." Woven from the wool of a Himalayan goat called cashmere, which is the popular spelling of Kashmir, the Kashmir shawl required a great deal of labor to produce it; hence it was expensive and acquired a regal cachet.

British weaving mills converted the woolen Kashmir style to mechanized cotton looms at the beginning of the nineteenth century. The most famous mills were those of Paisley in Scotland, which eventually substituted its name for the Kashmir shawl.

Kerosene Lighting

One of the greatest achievements of the Victorian period was its triumph over darkness. Electricity was only the last in a long line of Victorian lighting technologies. Like everything else the Victorians developed for the home, lighting had its class distinctions. Illustra-

Decorated faïence kerosene lamp by John Bennett, a former Doulton designer working in New York City, from Women's Handiwork in Modern Homes (1881).

tors of etiquette books, children's stories, adult literature, and periodicals like *Harper's Weekly* used lighting to distinguish between mansion and villa interiors illuminated with gas and cottage interiors lit by kerosene.

Victorian home decoration guides ignored kerosene, implying that those who couldn't afford gas wouldn't appreciate and couldn't afford the advice contained within. The frontispiece of *American Woman's Home* (1869) by Beecher and Stowe, which has been called "the bible of Victorian domesticity," sums up the situation nicely. The scene is that votive image of Victorian domesticity: the family circle. Three generations are gathered together in the living room reading by gaslight.

Kerosene lamps were often decorative as well as functional. As such, they are welcome additions to the Victorian interior.

Although kerosene lighting never cracked the top level of Victorian society, it was available in a broad range of fixtures, from hand-held, pressed-glass lamps with plain chimneys to elaborate metal six- and eight-unit chandeliers with milk glass globes ornamented in colored designs. Kerosene parlor lamps were available with richly sculptured bases and fonts, but the most beautiful were the multiple-layered, colored, cut-glass bases and fonts made of Sandwich glass. Today the technique is called overlay glass, but Victorians called it single-plated for two layers of glass and double-plated for three.

The most famous Victorian kerosene lamps are the parlor lamps of the 1880s that a Hollywood set designer used in the 1860s setting of the movie *Gone With the Wind.* Ever since, they have been known as Gone-With-the-Wind lamps, or simply GWTW lamps.

Further Reading: Kaiser, Joan E. and Barlow, Raymond E. *A Guide to Sandwich Glass: Kerosene Lamps and Accessories* (Windham, NH: Barlow-Kaiser Publishing, 1989). *Victorian Lighting: The Dietz Catalogue* (Watkins Glen, NY: American Life Books, 1982). Color facsimile of popular early 1860s catalog of kerosene fixtures. Freeman, Larry. *New Light on Old Lamps* (Watkins Glen, NY: American Life Books, 1984).

Kitchens

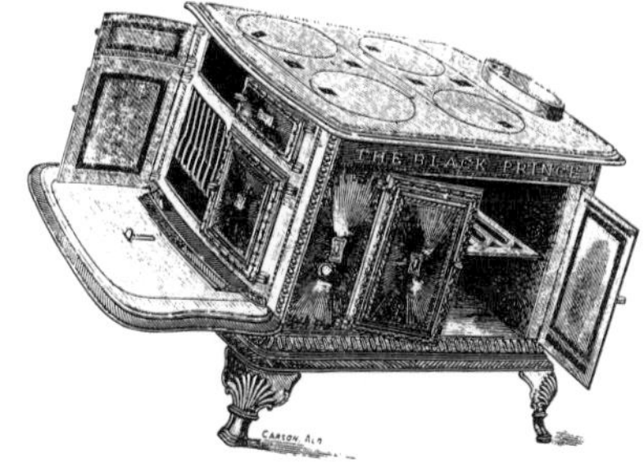

Isabella Beeton intended no pun in her famous *Book of Household Management* (1861) when she called the Victorian kitchen "the great laboratory of every household," but it was a great *labor*-atory in which the best labor-saving device was hired female help. Victorian domestic guidebooks constantly told how to decorate drawing-rooms and bedrooms, but seldom said anything about improving kitchens.

Late Victorian ladies decorated their kitchens in the same way they enlivened other rooms of their homes: with flowers, vines, and needlework. Even so, few kitchens were decorated up to the same level as a parlor or dining room.

Victorian Revival kitchens are frequently decorated with obsolete but venerable stoves, iceboxes, and butter churns along with defunct but country-cute agricultural artifacts like chicken cages and egg crates. Nearly all of these antiques-shop finds date only to the early twentieth century and are not genuinely Victorian at all.

It's possible to create a Victorian kitchen without a load of barnyard antiques and also make it a functional space. For example,

This is probably what the majority of Victorian kitchens in the country looked like, minus the paraphernalia required for actual use.

Though this is a parlor stove, used mostly for heat, it shows the beautiful detailing with which all appliances were decorated in Victorian times.

rather than storing kitchenware in expensive cabinetry, it's more economical and Victorian to store these items on open shelves. An abundance of genuine Victorian crockery and porcelain is available at auctions and antiques dealers for fractions of what their modern equivalents would cost. Display them on your open shelves or plate rails, and relegate any items you don't use to the basement or attic.

An authentic Victorian kitchen should have exposed storage—with tools and appliances arranged for maximum convenience and orderly ranks of jars filled with natural ingredients—as well as no curtains. Although it is certainly not a hi-tech environment, such a room can be quite charming. Great meals are more likely to be fondly remembered than the kitchens in which they were prepared. The best kitchens are designed and used to make good food instead of a good impression.

Language of the Flowers

Although generally regarded today as "typically Victorian," the language of the flowers was not invented by Victorians. "Saying it with flowers" was an ancient practice revived by Victorians—a natural extension of their passions for sentimental poetry and floral decoration.

Victorian floral dictionaries, often handsomely illustrated with color plates, listed the flowers and their associated meanings.

A BRIEF FLORAL DICTIONARY

Here is a selection of floral messages from *Flora's Interpreter* by Sarah Josepha Hale, famous editor of *Godey's Lady's Book*. First published in 1833, this book was enormously popular and went through many, many editions. These selections are from the 1837 edition, the year Queen Victoria took the throne.

Flower	*Message*
Damask red rose	*Bashful love*
Amaryllis	*Beautiful but timid*
Dandelion	*Coquetry*
Variegated tulip	*Beautiful eyes*
Narcissus	*Egotism, self love*
French marigold	*Jealousy*
White rose	*"I am in despair."*
Larkspur	*Fickleness*
Scarlet poppy	*Fantastic extravagance*

Because variety was the Victorian spice of life, bouquets were rarely made from one kind of flower. Our contemporary practice of handing over a dozen long-stemmed roses in a box would be regarded by proper Victorians as a primitive romantic gesture. By assembling bouquets of flowers that carried specific messages, while also harmonizing their shapes and colors, Victorians elevated bouquet-making into a fine art.

At a time when marriage was the highest institution in which women could seek membership, the complex romantic messages of bouquets often played the role of love letters. Because floral sentiments allowed several shades of meaning, the language of flowers provided more room for genteel maneuvering than words on paper, although when rejection was required the message had to be unequivocal.

By the late nineteenth century, abridged floral dictionaries were used as advertising premiums. This put the Victorian language of flowers into mass circulation and provided the means by which anyone who could read could translate the sentiments of bouquet picture postcards and send them long distances.

Lawn Party

One of the most accessible of Victorian entertainments is the lawn party. Don't be put off by surviving photographs, prints, and paintings of formal Victorian lawn parties. Victorians tended to dress for garden parties with clothing as ponderous and uncomfortable as that for indoor events. They did so because gardens were designed as outdoor parlors, in which the same stringent rules of indoor dress and decorum prevailed.

If the lawn party was restricted to socializing and eating, everyone was condemned to wear full formal dress. However, if lawn games like croquet, tennis, bowling, and archery were offered, players would not have been discouraged from shedding their coats and jackets and rolling up their sleeves. The invention of the sneaker in 1868 was evidence of such practicality. The first sneaker combined Charles Goodyear's vulcanized rubber for a sole with a canvas upper. Quite expensive, they quickly became fashionable for lawn parties and were called croquet sandals. If anyone criticizes you for showing up at a Victorian Revival lawn party dressed in white linen and wearing a pair of simple, clean, white sneakers, tell them they are Victorian croquet sandals and inquire as to the whereabouts of the game.

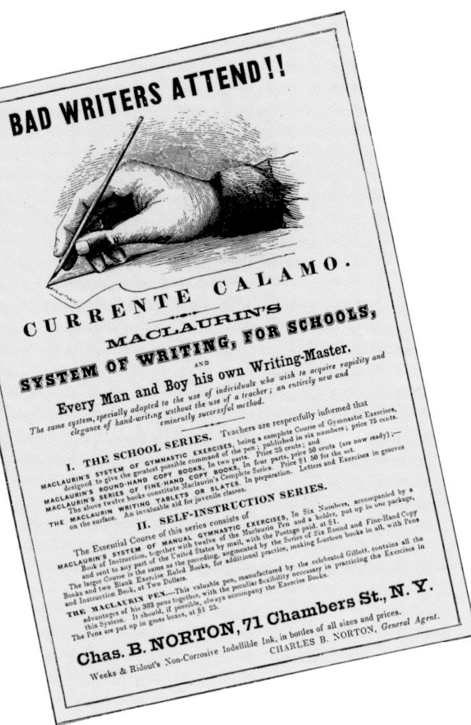

LETTERING

Penmanship, or "having a fine hand," was a much-admired accomplishment for Victorian gentlemen as well as ladies. Teachers of lettering enjoyed higher social stature than teachers of art because beautiful letters were considered to have more practical value. Penmanship guidebooks were more prevalent than drawing books.

An important Early Victorian teacher of lettering was the Boston engraver and printer Nathaniel Dearborn. I am pleased to own the copy of his *American Text Book for Letters* (1842), which he presented to his teacher Charles Folsom. In addition to an everyday "running hand," Dearborn shows how to use Hogarth's famous eighteenth-century "line of beauty" to make the elegant round hand best-known today as copperplate; it was so called because it was used for the text of eighteenth-century copperplate engravings.

Copperplate and other script styles shown by Dearborn—Old English, German Text, Engrossing Alphabet, Italian Alphabet—have enjoyed a renaissance recently as a personal art form. Lettering as a public art form has not been revived and perhaps never will because computer graphics do it inexpensively and more quickly.

It is possible to add Victorian "ornamented capitals" and other fancy letters of Dearborn's text book to a computer database, but the substance of their collective proportions, scale, spacing, and graphic color cannot be captured by the computer and activated to make words. When ornamental Victorian letters are used today for Victorian Revival books, magazine articles, posters, plaques, and signs, they often appear as collections of densely spaced, underscaled, and illegible words. Just as gingerbread details originally belonged to systems of designing buildings, Victorian lettering was part of a grand tradition. Revival of this lettering cannot seriously honor the Victorian period or be effective unless its practitioners understand entire alphabet systems. (*See also Monogams*)

Further Reading: Callingham, James. *Sign-Writing* (1870). The best guide to making Victorian letters for signs and posters, available in a reprint from American Life Books, Watkins Glen, NY.

Library

More so than art on the wall, which many pragmatic Victorians had difficulty justifying, culture in the Victorian home was represented by music and literature. At the lower end of the scale, it was reduced to a cheap pump organ and a small shelf filled with a decorated-cloth collected edition of popular authors like Sir Walter Scott or Charles Dickens. In wealthier homes, culture might have been expressed by a grand piano and harp in a music room and a library filled with leather-bound books.

Beginning in the 1870s, as Victorian resistance to art weakened under the pressure of the Aesthetic Movement, libraries also became galleries of art and museums of curiosities decorated with colorful leaded-glass sashes, richly figured drapes, densely patterned wallpapers, and an elaborate mantel for the obligatory, but obsolete, fireplace.

Clarence Cook, in his The House Beautiful (1878) wrote: "We want to have our books in our living room, and we want pictures and 'objects' and furniture, and comfort, too."

Linens

Linen did not fare well when the the manufacture of textiles became mechanized during the Victorian era, but it was and still is the fiber of choice for summer sheets, tablecloths, napkins, and lace—hence the generic term "linens" being used today to refer to those items whether they are made of linen or not. (*See also Fabrics*) Linens also graced the dining table. (*See also Dining Room*)

Due to its unsurpassed whiteness when bleached, formal table linens were white for most of the Victorian period. Tinted linens

Linen, lace, china, and crystal will enrich any table. The Victorian table was never without adornment.

became fashionable for special occasions late in the period, especially for "color teas," at which a color theme dominated the decorations. Surviving sets of fringed Victorian linen in delicate colors were reserved for tea parties. During the late nineteenth century, aesthetic hostesses draped their tables with colorful, patterned undercloths, but often topped them with a smaller white linen or white lace cloth set parallel to the undercloth or at an angle.

Linen napkins for ordinary Victorian dinners were folded in a simple manner to create a pocket containing the sliced piece of bread used as a knife rest and sop. Don't despair if your budget or inheritance hasn't bestowed your Victorian dining table with a glittering array of expensive silver, porcelain, and lead crystal. Bring the origami-like art of Victorian napkin-folding into play using a set of large, carefully washed, starched, and well-ironed linen napkins. Europeans call napkins serviettes, and *Fritzche's Illustriertes Servietten-Album,* a Late Victorian European hotel trade publication, showed how to make 122 designs for dinner using ordinary linen and 16 for tea using fringed linen.

It's tempting to select one of the elaborate Victorian designs that were often stuffed into a wine glass or water goblet. They were dramatically elevated above the plane of the table, but they tended to be over-scaled in relation to the glass as well as dangerously top-heavy. It's more practical—and equally attractive—to create contemporary designs with napkin rings. It's fun to collect distinctive napkin rings ornamented with plant and animal motifs. They will add a whimsical air to your dining table and delight family and guests, especially if you associate specific motifs—such as eagles or dogs—with specific people.

Further Reading: Kalish, Susan. *The Art of Napkin Folding: Completing the Elegant Table* (Philadelphia: Running Press, 1988).

Mantels, Fireboxes, Overmantels, and Chimneys

A handsome mantelpiece is the instant focal point of any room in which it is installed.

Late Victorian metal stoves and central heating made fireplaces obsolete, but you wouldn't have known it from the increasingly elaborate decoration of new fireboxes, mantels, overmantels, and chimneys. The symbolism of ancestral hearths was monumentalized by transforming them into mini-museums of decorative arts from many periods and many places. Oriental fans, tiles, ceramics, rare woods and veneers, leaded stained glass, mismatched candles, and sconces were arranged atop the mantel and around the hearth for an "aesthetic" effect.

The firebox area, when not in use as the flue for a metal parlor stove, was sometimes covered by a decoratively painted fireboard. Alternatives were a large vase of dried flowers or a large, opened, perforated brass fan. When it eventually became an occasional place for romantic and ceremonial flames generated by a gas-fired, cast-iron set of fake logs, the firebox area was decorated with tiles, cast-iron firebacks, brass andirons, and brass fenders, some of which used Aesthetic Movement motifs like the sunflower.

Chimneys were exposed on the outside for their entire lengths, rose high above the rooflines, and were ornamented by tiles, bas-relief terra-cotta panels, and fancy brickwork.

Victorian designers even paid attention to functional chimneys. These smokestacks are an integral part of elaborate mansardic design of the Hackley House in Muskegon, Michigan.

Marbling, Graining, and Gilding

Embellishing surfaces was a favorite technique of the Victorian decorative painter. Graining and marbling consisted of colored layers and lines of paint applied to inexpensive softwoods to imitate elegant and expensive hardwood and veined marbles.

Sir Walter Scott, according to Francis Litchen's *Decorative Art of Victoria's Era* (1950), was responsible for encouraging what became the characteristic Victorian use of wood-graining to imitate old

Marbling, or faux marble, is enjoying a revival for the same reason Victorian decorators used it—it creates grandeur at a low cost. This view of the Bellvue-Stratford's lobby in Philadelphia reveals the imitation of accidental effects essential to excellent marbling. The only decorative artists capable of achieving this are those who do it on a regular basis. That is why marbling and its sister art, graining, should be left to professional artists. The most common Victorian use of marbling was converting cheap slate into variegated marble mantelpieces.

woodwork. While he was decorating his famous Abbotsford during the 1820s, his demands for real medieval woodwork exceeded the available supply. He instructed his Edinburgh decorator—David Ramsay Hay, who later became a house painter and decorator to Queen Victoria—to blend the missing links between Gothic woodwork with "antiqued" Gothic Revival woodwork.

Gilding was most often used in small areas. It rarely imitated objects of solid gold. In Victorian decoration, gilding was chiefly used as a neutral color between patterns and areas of positive color. It was prevalently used in picture frames. Christopher Dresser's *Principles of Decorative Design* (1873) says, "The pictorial artist frames his pictures with gold because it, being a neutral, does not interfere with the tints of his work." He could have added that a gilded frame of the proper proportions also neutralizes colors of art within the frame and colors of walls outside the frame.

Mirrors

Victorian interiors without mirrors is a contradiction in terms. The most famous are the tall, gilded-frame, single-piece, French-plate, beveled-edge, High Victorian, overmantel mirrors. One can document the shift from High Victorian to Late Victorian interior decoration through overmantel mirrors. High Victorian ones tended to be large and were displayed for their own beauty as well as to reflect the decor on the opposite walls of the room. Late Victorian ones were small and functioned as backdrops to shelved objets d'art, reflecting their colors.

A fashionable Victorian parlor without a fancy fireplace was as unthinkable as a mantelpiece without an over-mantel mirror. The Mid-Victorian parlor of the Farnsworth House in Rockland, Maine, illustrates the essentials: marble-topped center table set for tea, wall-to-wall carpet, lace curtains, damask drapes with tasselled tie-backs, wooden valances, gilt-framed oil paintings hung from visible cords run over porcelain-headed nails driven through a wallpaper cornice border, and an easel holding an elaborate gilt-framed charcoal portrait with an artfully draped paisley scarf, a gas chandelier, and much more.

Monograms

Monograms are an old, aristocratic technique of identifying property; bourgeois Victorians adopted them with enthusiasm. Quickly programmed sewing machines capable of making three letters in sequence have restricted most of today's monograms to shirts, blouses, bath towels, and luggage. They have also degraded the art of the monogram to a somewhat banal level.

During the nineteenth century, monograms were primarily an engraver's art used on precious metals as well as engraved stationery. Designing monograms was the acme of the lettering art because a complete understanding of each letter in the alphabet was required before they could be overlaid and combined without the loss of legibility.

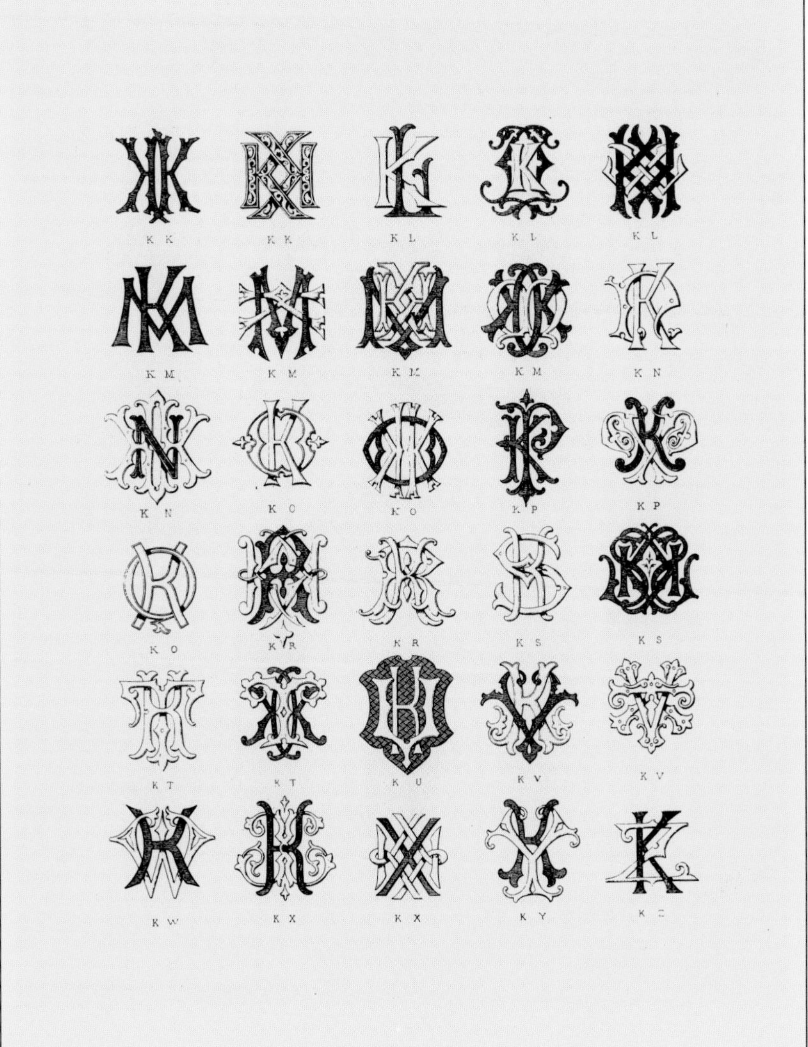

Graphic inventiveness is characteristic of Victorian monograms, often at the sacrifice of readability. For example, the one above requires a designed-in key at the bottom to identify and sequence the letters. To the left, a page from a Late Victorian engraver's "swipe book" shows various ways two letters can be arranged by reversals, doubling, rotation, changing scale, and black-on-white.

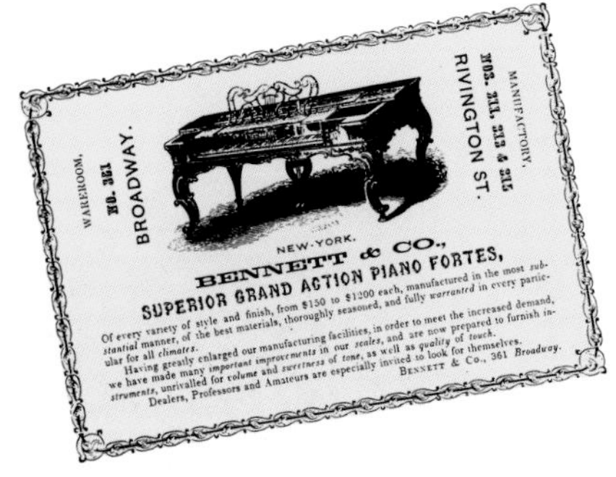

MUSIC

The most popular fine art of the Victorian period was music. If a family did not possess at least one "accomplished lady" or man who could play a musical instrument or sing, there were those in the neighborhood or village who could be invited and prevailed upon to provide an evening's musical entertainment. In some locales, the proverbial singing for one's supper was a practical necessity.

Nothing conjures up the Victorian period more efficiently and powerfully than Victorian music. Appreciating the works of Victorian concert-hall composers perhaps requires the skills of a musicologist, but the popular songs of the period can be enjoyed by anyone who enjoys music, be they Sousa marches, Strauss waltzes, or Gilbert and Sullivan patter songs.

Some of the most influential publications of the British Aesthetic Movement were children's books produced by Marcus Ward. This accomplished little lady, shown in At Home Again, has put the bay window of this simple parlor to good use as a naturally lit place to practice. The point of the poem that goes with it is that the violin makes music "better than music ever heard, from flower or tree, of bee or bird."

NEEDLEWORK

Decorative needlework was occupational therapy for Victorian ladies of leisure during long hours spent in their homes. This art allowed women to adorn themselves and their interiors with their own handiwork. Although many forms of Victorian decorative needlework have been revitalized by the modern crafts movement, its abundant use in Victorian interiors has not been revived. Few have the leisure or patience today to make it in great quantity, and a few pieces are sufficient to remind anyone that these notorious dust-catchers are difficult to keep clean.

Victorian decorative needlework is a wonderful collectible, especially for anyone who has attempted the various techniques. It is often neglected and underpriced at sales and auctions.

The arts of drawing and collage have been combined to create this charming "now I lay me down to sleep and perchance to dream" pillow sham.

Newel Posts

Despite the prevalence of single-story ranch houses in late twentieth century America, the two-story home is widespread and owned by familes of modest means. But the symbolic potency of Victorian newel posts, which justified their elaborate decoration, has been lost. Surviving originals are lovingly restored as the precious objects they were, but most Americans no longer associate the newel post with the Victorian social achievement of owning a two-story home.

Single-story cottages were designed for the basics of family living: a kitchen, multipurpose living room, and bedrooms. Multiple-story villas and mansions enabled bedrooms to be removed from the public first floor to the private floors above. These homes also featured a hallway which functioned as a holding area for guests as well as a circulation area to surrounding rooms and the floor above. A grand staircase terminating in an elaborate newel post was the symbolic as well as functional object that differentiated minimal shelter from elaborate residences.

Victorian newel posts, when they get as large and elaborate as this one, are the Alpha-and-Omega of the elegant staircase. The dark walnut and nicely figured veneers of this one are hidden under twentieth-century anti-Victorian white paint.

Nursery

During most of the Victorian period children were neither seen nor heard. For those who could afford it, children were banished to an in-house day-care center called the nursery under the benevolent tyranny of a nanny or governess. Girls suffered longer from the confinement of the nursery than boys, who were released to boarding school. Brilliant and less scholarly women alike had little choice

All it takes to make a romantic nursery is wicker furniture, eyelet lace, quilts, and a wallpaper cornice border. Reddish blues, like sapphire or cornflower, also make handsome nurseries for girls as well as boys.

but to accept the long-term imprisonment of the nursery system, which protected their flowerlike delicacy and innocence until men came along and plucked them into marriage.

Beatrix Potter endured long years in the nursery, and her frustration with it was partially resolved in her famous little books about animals with childlike personalities. These were originally written for young children visiting her family. Peter Rabbit and other animal stories eventually made enough money to buy her freedom from her parents as well as rescue her publisher from the ruin of embezzlement. Royalties from her books continue to support The National Trust, which she founded to protect the landscape of the Lake District in England.

At Home Again, a British Aesthetic Movement children's book, shows three captives in a Late Victorian nursery trying to escape by rocking and rolling to Fairyland. This three-seat rocker would be an excellent craft project for the home woodworker.

Victorian decorative arts of the nursery are almost entirely the product of the more relaxed and liberal attitude toward children under the visual leadership of artists associated with the Aesthetic Movement. Children's books illustrated by Kate Greenaway and Walter Crane, along with picture books published by Marcus Ward under the art direction of Crane's brother Thomas, were a global impetus to visual improvements in the nursery environment.

By the end of the period, all guidebooks and magazine series on home decoration included a section on making the nursery beautiful with special colors, textiles, furniture, and wallpapers. Late Victorian boys and girls of stylish parents were dressed in clothes imitating Kate Greenaway's romantic adaptations of adult Regency fashions for children. Perhaps one of the most pleasant aspects of the Victorian Revival is the recent popularity of such clothing for little girls.

Observatories

British eighteenth-century landscape gardening taught Victorians around the world the pleasures of enjoying what was called "the prospect," hence the need for an observatory on the roofs of Victorian villas and mansions. It was also called a cupola, widow's walk, and belvedere. Towers, turrets, bay windows, and gazebos served the same function to a lesser extent.

Fires, neglect, and economizing eventually destroyed many observatories, thereby visually injuring the architecture to which they were attached. Such buildings look like stories without a conclusion.

Observatories were more than platforms for looking at the landscape or star-gazing, they also were important components in the Victorian system of summer air conditioning using natural convection currents. Air cooled by surrounding trees and the shade of broad verandahs was sucked in through first-floor windows by interior hot air rising through a central hallway and shooting out the opened observatory windows. Anyone sitting on the verandahs would be cooled by the air being drawn into the house.

Longwood, at Natchez, Mississippi, is the best surviving example in America of fantasy-Mediterranean architecture in what its Philadelphia architect, Samuel Sloan, called the Moorish style—largely due to the onion-shaped dome of its observatory. It is also one of the largest surviving examples of a Victorian octagon house.

ORNAMENT BOOKS

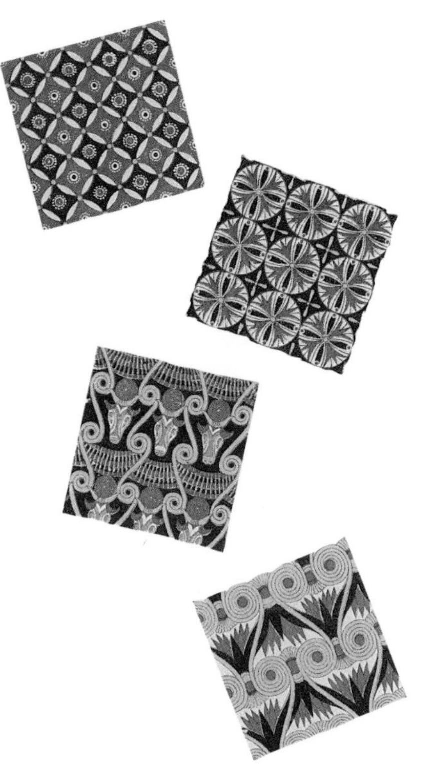

Although the Late Victorian ornamentalist William Morris is famous today for his patterns and books, the prince of the Victorian polychrome ornament was Owen Jones. He is best known for his magnum opus *The Grammar of Ornament* (1856). As one of the most important promoters of Victorian architectural polychrome, in 1850 he was appointed joint architect with Sir Joseph Paxton for the Crystal Palace exhibition building in London. He was responsible for its interior decoration. Although Owen Jones was capable of designing polychrome ornament in any style, he devoted a major portion of his career to Moorish and Egyptian designs.

It is not by accident that many of Jones's plates for *The Grammar of Ornament* look like designs for tiles. During the 1840s, he was chiefly known as a tile designer for Minton—a tile manufacturer—and others. He produced *Designs for Mosaic and Tesselated Pavements* in 1842 and *Encaustic Tiles* in 1843. During the years before his death in 1874, he designed tiles for Maw. (*See also Tiles*)

OUTHOUSES

Because my common first name is also a popular name for common outbuildings that the eighteenth century called "necessaries," I have been seized by a peculiar fascination for them. Many are still used in rural areas, especially at Pennsylvania Amish and Mennonite farmhouses and schoolhouses. It is difficult to distinguish a long-abandoned Victorian outhouse from similar shaped ice houses, spring houses, and smoke houses. A door with the crescent cutout, which a comedian named Chic Sale made famous in his twentieth-century vaudeville monologue, won't identify a Victorian outhouse either. A small cupola with louvers or open grillwork in the center of the roof serving as a ventilator is often the only outward sign. The unmistakable indicator appears inside: the seat or seats, counted off as "holers."

This outhouse in Chatham, Massachusetts, has been detailed in the Italianate style of the Victorian house to which it was a "necessary."

A handsome design for a Victorian three-holer with two seats for women and one for men, complete with porch in front and garden seat in the back, appears in *Villas and Cottages* (1857) by Calvert Vaux. His most famous architectural designs are those for New York City's Central Park, which he did in partnership with Frederick Law Olmsted. If your nose for Victorian romanticism doesn't include the "necessary" part of this easily built charmer, the three-holer could be converted to a toolshed or potting shed.

Further Reading: Barlew, Ronald S. *The Vanishing American Outhouse* (El Cajon, CA: Windmill Publishing, 1989).

Papier Mâché

For an age such as ours, as we search for ways to recycle discarded materials into useful objects, Victorian papier mâché merits serious consideration. Made from shredded scrap paper soaked in glue, it was the most decorative recycled product of its period. Papier mâché had been made in France since the eighteenth century and was manufactured in Britain. At the height of its development it was

A papier-mâché spoon-back chair with inlaid mother-of-pearl decorations, made in England, circa 1840.

displayed at the Crystal Palace exhibition of 1851 and was revived in the 1870s as a home craft or fancy work. The most common example was a small black table with a tilt top containing the characteristic decoration of glass beads, glass jewels, and mother-of-pearl. The moonlit landscape was also a favorite subject, in addition to floral designs.

Parlors

No single room of a Victorian house has been more maligned than the parlor, especially the Late Victorian parlor—which functioned as a gloriously cluttered and exceedingly upholstered minimuseum of arts and artifacts from all over the world. The memories of Late Victorian children were the primary source of parlor vilification during the early twentieth century. They said they detested parlors for several reasons. The parlor was the only room in their home where children were routinely treated as dangerous intruders. Parlors were filled with wonderful curiosities children were forbidden to touch except upon special, adult-supervised occasions. During rare, sanctioned appearances of children in parlors, they were dressed in their most uncomfortable clothes and were warned to be on their best behavior. The parlor was also used for home funerals. Long after that ceased to be practical or fashionable, undertakers continued to call their place of business a "funeral parlor."

The parlor was the best room of the house, dedicated to social conversation—as its derivation from *parler,* the French word for speaking, indicates. It was the tangible reminder that a family had arrived at a middle-class station in Victorian life and was prepared to receive "society" unannounced at any time. A disproportionate amount of disposable income went into the decoration of the parlor—often income that was not disposable, to the peril of the family finances. It was here that fashion wreaked havoc on a regular basis.

Early Victorian interior decoration has its roots in the Regency and Empire styles of the early nineteenth century, as seen in the example to the left. The famous frontispiece from Clarence Cook's The House Beautiful of 1878 is a good example of the Aesthetic mode that, unfortunately, dwindled into the infamous eclectic clutter of the late nineteenth century. For example of a Mid-Victorian parlor, see page 102.

Pictures: Framing and Hanging

Perhaps there is no aspect of Victorian interior decoration for which people today are more ill-prepared than the selection, framing, and hanging of period pictures. Few things look more out of place in a Victorian Revival interior than contemporary works displayed in twentieth-century fashion.

For those who can afford them, original Victorian colored prints and paintings have always been available. But monochromatic Victorian engravings and lithographs, which are often affordable, tend to be rejected as candidates for framing and hanging. Several enterprises have sprung up recently that supply colorful prints at a reasonable cost. Honest facsimiles of prints are preferrable to engravings and lithographs ripped out of bound Victorian books and periodicals—a despicable practice that has been going on for many years, destroying in the process countless Victorian texts that are thereafter discarded as useless. Amateurish coloring of these prints not only is dishonest but destroys their subtle graphic qualities.

The simple black-and-white elegance of this picture frame was characteristic of the short-lived British Aesthetic Movement during the 1870s and 1880s. It deserves to be revived. Wooden frames were first coated with plaster-of-paris and then painted with gloss black. The elegantly placed patterns were carved to reveal the plaster under the paint.

Most Victorian prints were simply inserted without matting into frames scaled to the size of the print and ornamented to harmonize with the prevailing decor. The chief visual function of gilding was to interpose a neutral color between the positive colors of the artwork and the wall. (*See also Marbling, Graining, and Gilding*)

Owners of Victorian homes are often reluctant to use the picture moldings at the bottom of their cornices or the picture rails beneath their cornices properly because it would expose the inverted Vs from which the picture frames are suspended. However, this was a commonsense Victorian practice.

Perhaps some of what E.C. Gardner's *Home Interiors* (1878) says about what he considered the old-fashioned method of hanging pictures will be familiar to you. "Pound the plaster all around the room to find a spot that gives a solid sound, then punch holes with a scratch-awl all around it, in the hope of finding a stud, driving a nail or screwing a screw into the crack between two springing laths and finally trusting a heavy gilt frame and big sheet of glass to the treacherous support of crumbling mortar."

Picture rails protected the walls of Victorian homes from the weight of properly framed Victorian pictures and the injury of nails or screws. Furthermore, because Victorians were constantly adding new pictures, frames were frequently rearranged on the wall—a practice that would have made the wall eventually look like Swiss cheese if it were not for the picture rails. To avoid the look of "a gallows whereon pictures are to be hung," Gardner said it was "just as easy and ten times more delightful to make picture rails a component part of the essential work, either of the constructive casing and cornices, or of the color decoration, or of both."

Victorians ornamented picture wires by wrapping them with colorful threads or by inserting them into a hollow cord. If such wires were attached to the picture by a brass S-shaped hook, a handsome tassel was sometimes suspended from the hook.

Lincoln's home in Springfield, Illinois, has pictures hung in the Mid-Victorian style. Note the porcelain-headed nails, cloth-covered wires, and picture-nail tassels. Note the freshly gilded mantelpiece garniture called girondoles with bas-relief sculptures illustrating an episode from the story of Paul and Virginia. The best fantasy piece is the cast-iron parlor stove, which looks like a quilted tent on cabriole legs!

Plaster: Decorative

One of the highly skilled class of decorative artists prevalent during the Victorian period was the maker of ornamental plaster. This skill has nearly disappeared during the twentieth century. They "ran" all of the cornices, made and set the panel moldings for walls and ceilings, and made and set the ceiling rosettes or centerpieces. During the period, decorators could purchase all of these plaster decorations in precast form out of catalogs, but many architect-designed buildings required the artistry of an ornamental plasterer.

Precast plaster decorations are still available from catalogs, in addition to copies of them in modern materials like fiberglass and styrene.

Source: David Flaharty, 402 Magazine Road, RD 2, Green Lane, PA 18054. Skilled craftsman and restorer of ornamental plasterwork.

Portrait medallions dominate the restored ceiling of the Curtis House in Saratoga Springs, New York.

Pompeii

Today it is difficult to appreciate the impact made by the nineteenth-century excavations of Pompeii and Herculaneum, two time capsules of Ancient Roman life buried by the eruption of Mt. Vesuvius in 79 AD. These discoveries were responsible for the revival of the painted wall in the Empire styles of France and Britain. When

This hallway is from the Livingstone County Courthouse, Howell, Michigan.

the British Aesthetic Movement revived the Empire style in the late nineteenth century, Pompeiian decorations became part of the stylistic baggage exported to America in the 1870s and 1880s. The biggest impact of Pompeiian decorations upon Victorian interior design was the division of the Late Victorian wall surface into dado, fill, and frieze. The most enduring contribution of Pompeiian decoration is a wall color called Pompeiian red.

Portières

E.C. Gardner's *Home Interiors* (1878) condemns interior doors with fervor typical of Late Victorian decorating guides. "If I should ever be sat upon by coronors, I think the verdict will be 'died of doors.' They worry me beyond measure. The square, stiff, selfish, inhospitable things!" The Late Victorian substitute for interior doors was a heavy drape made from luxurious and richly colored fabrics, sometimes embroidered, to which was attached the fancy French name *portière.*

The best promotion of portières appears in Constance Cary Harison's *Woman's Handiwork in Modern Homes* (1881), in which

The portière at the entrance of this Mid-Victorian parlor is more functional than decorative so that it doesn't compromise the splendid valance and pier mirror behind it.

she justifies it for its associations with the tabernacle of Moses, "all the glittering phantasmagoria of the Arabian Nights," and "a waft from 'far Cathay.'" After stating the general rule that "the portière should not repeat the curtains of a room," she lists the fashionable colors in plush and velveteen, which are available as backgrounds for embroidered portières. The collection is a psychedelic experience: "seal-brown, nut-brown and fawn; old gold, orange, maize, amber; garnet, wine color, pomegranate, Indian-red, crushed strawberry; peacock, turquoise, celestine, drake's neck, Damascus blue and robin's-egg blue; olive, sage, myrtle, jasper and resedas or mignonette green."

An antidote for today's fashion of puddled-and-poofed draperies is her comment: "Never commit the vulgar error of making your draperies too full or too long. They should be scant enough to display the design, and should touch, not trail upon, the floor."

Portières could be decorated on both sides to match the room they faced, thereby solving the old problem of swinging a door with one woodwork color into a room with another woodwork color.

Single-piece portières made from a new textile or an antique one like a Kashmir shawl were the easiest to make and required the least thought. The cleverest portières were careful selections of different materials positioned to carry the Late Victorian horizontal wall divisions across the entrances to a room. The chief attraction of portières was this capacity to recycle an odd assortment of old fabrics combined more on the basis of their colors than their fibers, antiquity, patterns, or places of origin. The best examples combined exquisite textiles imaginatively; the worst ones had a disorderly, patchwork quality.

QUILTS

This delightful example of a crazy quilt from the collections of the Shelburne Museum remarkably combines pictorial elements with a background of crazy quilt collage.

Folk art and the American Country style have been so closely associated with American quilts throughout the twentieth century that it can come as a bit of a shock to collectors, dealers, and quilters that many of the finest American appliqué and patchwork quilts are Victorian. The sewing circle, the quilting frolic, the friendship quilt, and the album quilt were some of the Victorian traditions that preserved and enhanced the seventeenth- and eighteenth-century English tradition of quilting through the nineteenth century.

Pennsylvania Germans during the 1850s started making quilted cotton bedcoverings instead of their traditional woven wool coverlets. The tradition developed and has been maintained among the Amish and Mennonite communities to such an extent that they are today's chief source of American-made quilts.

It was easy enough to pass off most Victorian quilts as Early American or folk art or American Country, but one variety was agressively Victorian: the crazy quilt. First popular during the 1880s, and promoted by manufacturers of silk embroidery thread who were the chief beneficiaries of the style, crazy quilts had the same relation to traditional patchwork as the Queen Anne style did to traditional Victorian architecture. Both explored and reveled in materials for their own sake; both were creative self-expressions; both had an adolescent quality.

In her *Decorative Art of Victoria's Era* (1950) Francis Lichten draws from her own memories to state, "Children adored crazy-quilts, not only for the [adult stories about the memories associated with the different pieces of fabric] which accompanied their display, but especially for the pictorial [silk embroidery] needlework with which they were covered."

Although quilts require needlework skills for piecing and decorative quilting, the chief artistic attraction of quilt-making remains the selection of colored pattern fabrics and their placement in a mosaic pattern. Unlike the crazy quilt, which displayed the inherent beauties of various fabrics in amorphous shapes, the textile patterns,

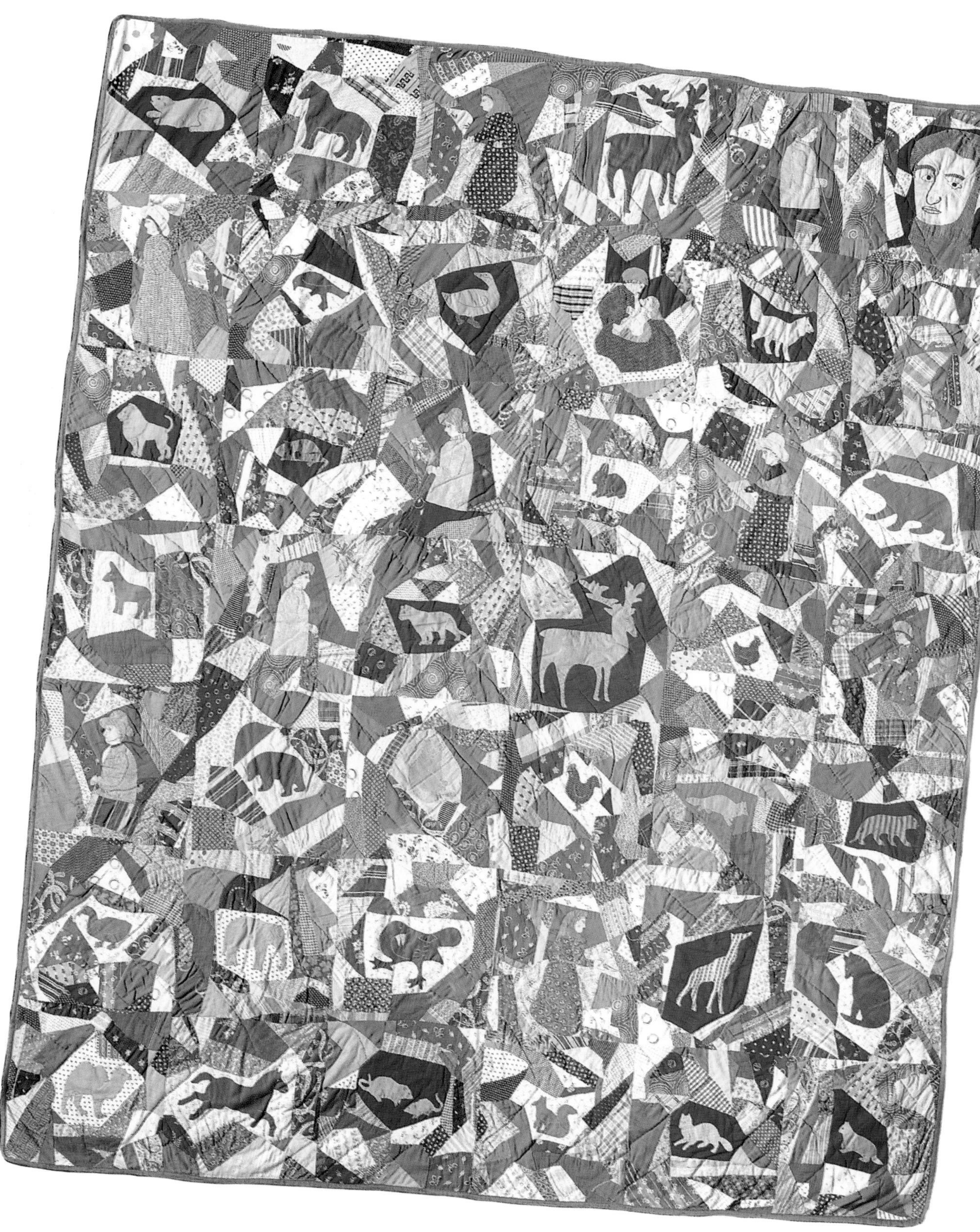

colors, and textures used in Victorian patchwork and appliqué quilts were subservient to the mosaic of the quilt pattern.

Victorian quilts were symbolic artifacts of domesticity. They were given as wedding presents and used as bedcoverings.

Sources: Judy Freeman, P.O. Box 430, Norristown, PA 19404 (215) 539-3010. A custom quilt designer and consultant skilled in the Victorian traditions.

Another crazy quilt from the Shelburne Museum is an example of the Late Victorian style dominated by richly colored silk embroidery thread stitches joining the pieces. Manufacturers of silk thread created and promoted these "crazy quilt stitches."

RAILROAD

The most spectacular Victorian transportation invention was the railroad, even though the automobile was invented toward the end of the period. Nothing has superseded the railroad in efficiently moving tonnage across terrain. As urban and suburban roadways become more choked with automobiles and concern for the environment increases, interurban railroads may well regain the importance they had in the Victorian era.

Many of the most fashionable communities surrounding major cities were originally real estate developments of Victorian railroad companies. For example, the Pennsylvania Railroad converted farm acreage and villages with names like Hogtown along its Main Line outside Philadelphia into Victorian landscaped suburbs with romantic Welsh names like Bryn Mawr. One of them filled with architect-designed Queen Anne homes has the oldest active civic improvement society: The North Wayne Protective Association.

There are a number of narrow-gauge railroads, railroad museums, and special railroad excursion companies that romanticize Victorian steam engine railroads. Unfortunately, I am old enough to recall the last of the steam engines spewing damaging smoke and scattering sparks that started grass fires, one of which nearly torched my family's Greek Revival home in rural New York State. Even so, a ride on any train never fails to excite me.

My peak experience in railroading happened when Dane and Joan Wells—owners of the famous Queen Victoria Inn at Cape May, New Jersey—included my family in a private railway car excursion to Colonial Williamsburg in Virginia. We dressed formally in the Victorian style for dinner. The amenities were summed up by an engraved brass plaque on the wall of the dining room, which quoted Mrs. August Belmont's remark, "One does not have to learn how to appreciate a private railroad car; one takes to it immediately."

Sources: Private Varnish. Includes listings of owners of private railroad cars who rent them for excursions.

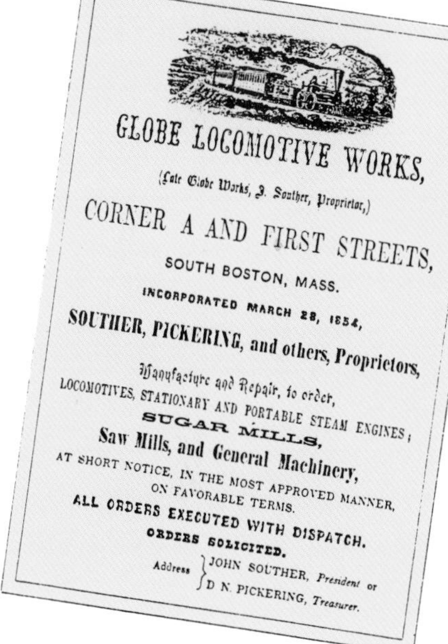

Roller Shades

One of the lost arts of Victorian interior decoration that merits consideration for revival is the painted roller shade. Most of them were made in the home by one of the methods of Victorian fancy work. Early Victorian practitioners of this art painted romantic landscapes with decorative borders on cotton cloth. When they were drawn down during the day for shade, sunlight brought these unwound pictures to life. In the evening when they were drawn down for privacy, artificial back-lighting transformed them into magic lantern slides seen from the street. A large vase filled with flowers was also a favorite design.

Late Victorians abandoned the landscape and flower painting of translucent roller shades in favor of richly colored dadoes on nearly opaque glazed cotton called Holland cloth. Here are the colors from a swatch book of the period: chamois, dark ecru, brown, linnet, green, windsor sage, nile green, fern, laurel, spanish olive, blue, white, bronze, old gold, puce, light bronze, palmetto. The principle behind them was carrying the color scheme and decoration of the walls across the windows when the roller shades were in use.

Both styles of roller shade were products of their time. Early Victorian examples were designed to unite interiors with exteriors. Late Victorian examples were designed to unify interiors. Early ones celebrated landscapes and flowers. Late ones celebrated interior decoration.

The color range of roller shade cloth is now limited to unappealing yellow and green, as well as white. Yet cloth manufactured for the binding of books can be converted into Late Victorian dado roller shades. Any translucent cotton material can be treated and painted to make Early Victorian landscape and floral roller shades.

Colored roller blinds, sometimes in two colors front and back, continued to be popular into the 1920s. There was proper concern for how they looked inside and out. During the day outside light would lighten the dark inside color and at night artificial light would bring it to life, especially if there were any gilt patterns.

Most decorated roller shades were worn out with use. This rare Mid-Victorian survivor is from the collection of the American Life Foundation.

Rugs and Carpets

Victorians had more of a love-hate relationship with carpets than any other aspect of interior decoration. Harriet Beecher Stowe's 1864 *House and Home Papers* begins with "The Ravages of a Carpet"—an amusing story about the consequences of a comfortable mid-Victorian family purchasing a new carpet for their parlor. The canary was banished to the kitchen because he was a messy eater. The plants followed because they dropped dead blossoms and leaves and the pots leaked and might break. "In a year we had a

This Mid-Victorian bedroom is dominated by an ingrain carpet with its sewn-together strips visible. If you were looking at this room during that period, you would wonder when the decorative painter or paper hanger was coming to do something about the walls. Victorians were never shy about mixing different colors and patterns on their floors and walls.

parlor with new lounges in decorous recesses, a fashionable sofa, and six chairs and a looking-glass, and a fireplace always shut up, and a hole in the floor which kept the parlor warm, and great, heavy curtains that kept out all the light."

Victorian carpet anxiety was caused by the accumulated regal associations of hand-woven Asian and French rugs. After 1685, when Louis XIV revoked the tolerant Edict of Nantes, fleeing Protestant weavers reestablished their French skills in Holland, Germany, and England.

Kidderminster, which also eventually made Wilton or cut-pile carpets, became the center of the English Brussels carpet industry. The first Brussels loom was imported from the Continent in 1745 by a Kidderminster weaver named John Broom. A Scottish carpet industry was established in the 1830s, when tapestry, velvet, and chenille carpets were developed. The greatest development since the loom itself was both Victorian and American: Erastus B. Bigelow's invention of the power loom in 1839. The famous slogan that Bigelow used during the twentieth century—"A Title on the Door Rates a Bigelow on the Floor"—perfectly sums up the Victorian attitude toward carpets.

Oriental rugs, often used to define various functional areas of a room, were popular during the late nineteenth century. This interior shows how such a decorative treatment may be combined with the practicality of a modern wall-to-wall carpet in a light, semi-neutral hue. Note, too, the importance of the decorated screen to define this area.

Francis Lichten's *Decorative Art of Victoria's Era* (1950) mentions an Ohio pioneer settler of the 1840s who unintentionally made her neighbors feel socially inferior and kept them from calling on her because it was rumored she owned a Brussels carpet! She did, but "it had never even been unrolled, for life in a new village was too harsh and she would not subject her precious carpet to such rigors."

The most common Victorian carpet was ingrain, a name derived from an archaic term for yarns dyed "in the grain" prior to weaving. Because it was woven like a coverlet with the addition of one or more piles between the surfaces to stiffen it, ingrain carpets featured reversible patterns—quite a useful feature because they wore out rapidly.

Rugs and carpets are two terms which tend to be used interchangeably. When used with any precision, carpets cover the entire floor, and rugs cover a portion. This is conveyed in the contemporary redundancies of "wall-to-wall carpet" and "area rugs." The Victorian period can be divided coarsely in terms of floor coverings by the great shift in Victorian decoration that occurred during the 1870s. It was fashionable for Early Victorian floors to be covered with carpets; Late Victorian floors were decorated with rugs.

Late Victorians ridiculed the Early Victorian fondness for simulating interior flower gardens with gaudy floral carpets. These had been made since the 1830s. Late Victorians were obsessed with variety, so they objected to the Early Victorian penchant for decoration *en suite*: a single pattern covering the floor from wall-to-wall didn't satisfy their varied tastes.

The Arts and Crafts Movement taught Late Victorians to expose the "honest" and real beauties of wooden flooring instead of covering them up with the imitative beauty of carpeting. Late Victorian central heating made open planning possible, and rugs were selected and placed in such interiors to delineate subordinate areas within a large and complex flowing space. Rugs also functioned as behavior modifiers, indicating routes to take and places to stand.

Perhaps carpets were damned most because of the difficulty of cleaning them. In 1878, E.C. Gardner wrote in *Home Interiors,* "I only wish the enlightened savages who believe in wool carpets the year round were required to put them down and take them up each year, and hold the inquest on the remains." Carpets had to be untacked, rolled up, taken into the back yard, unrolled face down, and wolloped with a carpet beater—an instrument of torture to user and carpet alike. They didn't become fashionable again until the perfection of the vacuum cleaner by Hoover. Small, loose rugs were much easier to remove, reinstall, and clean with a carpet beater.

It is hopeless to search for antique Victorian rugs and carpets. Most of those that survive are faded and worn beyond further service. Pristine examples will meet the same fate if used. They should be donated to the nearest textile museum for safe keeping.

The implications of Harriet Beecher Stowe's little story should be considered before you invest in either carpets or rugs. The key question is, "What do we want to emphasize?" If you put a set of Late Victorian papers on the walls that makes people feel like they have walked into an oriental carpet and put an oriental carpet on the floor, the two will cancel each other out. People will swoon from aesthetic overload. Similarly, if you have elegant and richly upholstered furniture, a semi-neutral color on the walls and rugs with subtle details will create a harmonious setting. If your floors are so far gone they require hiding, a plain, semineutral carpet can be installed and rugs overlaid on the carpet.

Further Reading: Von Rosentiel, Helene and Winkler, Gail Caskey. *Floor Coverings for Historic Buildings* (Washington, DC: Preservation Press).

Rustic Adornments

The current vogue of twig chairs for gardens is a revival of Victorian rustic adornments. Natural, free materials—such as wood, pine cones, and seashells—were fashioned into useful objects at home, which saved Victorian families money.

The rustic motif was popular in the garden. Wooden ornaments were primarily associated with Victorian cottages, but even the most pretentious villa or mansion might have a rustic summer house, a couple of seats, and an arbor made out of intertwined, bark-covered branches located somewhere in the estate gardens.

Illustrations of these wooden rustic adornments survive in books, magazines, and photographs, but many cast-iron examples exist and continue to be produced, especially the grapevine bench. In small country towns and some sections of cities one can discover cast-iron rustic verandahs in the grapevine, wisteria, and barked branch styles that escaped wartime scrap drives. At the Philadelphia Centennial of 1876, the garden paths were lined by semi-circles of cast-iron bent branches.

Only a Victorian artist like Frederic Church would have the courage and ability to incorporate a rustic armchair in the midst of his library at Olana.

Rustic adornments invaded interiors as well and became favorite subjects of homemade Victorian fancy work. Perhaps the most popular was the twig frame, made from interlaced evergreens arranged in a Gothic Revival style. Another version was made from thin hardwood sticks carved to resemble bark, woven into a frame, and decorated at the corners with acorns or pine cones. Mosses, leaves, and shells were also used to decorate the surfaces of boxes, especially window boxes and other containers for flowers and ferns. They were also used on aquariums, terrariums, and bird cages.

The most charming examples of rustic adornments survive in Victorian graphic arts, especially title pages, initial letters, and vignettes. There were even display types drawn in bark-covered branches.

SCIENCE FICTION

Like most great science fiction, the *voyages imaginaires* of Jules Verne were prophetic. The French novelist, who lived from 1828 to 1905, is often called the father of modern science fiction. His immensely popular works of the 1860s and 1870s predicted such successful twentieth-century technologies as submarines, airplanes, rockets and space travel, and television. Among Verne's works were *Journey to the Center of the Earth* (1864), *Twenty Thousand Leagues Under the Sea* (1870), and *Around the World in Eighty Days* (1873).

The British writer H.G. Wells, who lived from 1866 to 1946, also sparked Late Victorian flights of scientific fantasy with *The Time Machine* (1895) and *The War of the Worlds* (1898).

Here is the Time Machine, as envisioned by H.G. Welles and executed in the 1960 movie.

Scrapbooks

The explosion of color in books, magazines, television, and videos today makes it difficult to appreciate how starved Victorian children were for color and how little it took to satisfy them.

Children left to their own devices without financial aid saved scraps of colored wrapping paper, fabric, and wallpaper for backgrounds and combined them with hand-tinted fashion plates from ladies' magazines like *Godey's,* calling cards, greeting cards, obsolete engravings from catalogs, and advertising trade cards to create imaginative scrapbooks.

Wealthy parents would finance buying sprees supervised by a governess in the local fancy store that stocked big and beautifully bound blank scrapbooks along with packets of chromolithographed, diecut, and embossed pictures in all of the favorite Victorian categories: flowers, bouquets, birds, pets, horses, wild animals, babies, cupids, ships, butterflies, fashion queens, fruits, fans, landscapes, and—after the Civil War—military heroes.

Descendants of Victorian embossed and diecut chromolithographs are today's stickers, but they are rarely arranged in the Victorian fashion on blank pages in a scrapbook. Spending money is not the way to revive the Victorian tradition of scrapbooks. Make a game out of spending as little as possible.

From the adult viewpoint, the best Victorian scrapbooks are like this one of the 1880s. Part of the collection of the American Life Foundation, this was obviously put together by children under adult supervision. Wesley Elliott and his siblings made numerous visits to a "fancy card" shop in Schenectady, New York, which—thanks to the financial support of their father—yielded this birthday gift for their mother, whose name was Lulu.

Befriend your local decorator or department store decorating department and ask for a gift of obsolete sample books featuring old-fashioned patterns in small scale. Prevail upon your local printer to give you some leftover sheets of stiff paper. It will surprise you what people are willing to do for children. Save pictures from magazines and catalogs. If you don't have embroidery scissors for precise cutting, you will have to buy them, but it is a minor expense. You can even make your own wheat paste to affix these pictures to the scrapbook pages.

Making a Victorian scrapbook with your children provides an opportunity for you to share your love for Victorian decoration with the next generation. Because children see the world differently, they will open your eyes as much as you open theirs. The key is to get them started, provide gentle direction at moments of frustration, quit when their attention span is over, and enjoy watching them arrange old things in a new way.

Screens

Screens require an improved reputation before they can be revived as a popular decorative element. Screens are associated today either with artist's models and actresses undressing or enormously expensive oriental examples in fancy interiors. But during the Victorian period screens of various kinds were practical as well as beautiful.

The smallest was the hand-screen, a popular gift item decorated at home on stiff paper, which ladies held before the delicate complexion of their faces as a shield against the glare of the fireplace. A larger and more pretentious version was a framed needlework scene, which could be adjusted in height on a pole set into a fancy base. A firescreen framing an elaborate needlework picture acted as a decorative cover for the fireplace when not in use.

Of all the Victorian screens, the most useful was the folding screen. Victorians did not invent it, nor was it popular throughout the period. By the 1870s, when it was revived, it was so old-fashioned as to have been virtually forgotten. *Home Interiors,* an 1878 guidebook by E.C. Gardner, said the chief practicality of a folding screen is that it "can be snugly banished whenever its room is more valuable than its company."

Gardner lists eight uses for folding screens: (1) Keep sun off a favorite carpet; (2) Block draughts of air; (3) Shade eyes from bright lights; (4) "Temporarily close draped openings that have no doors"; (5) "Concealing a door not often used, but which cannot be permanently abolished"; (6) "Dividing a large room into two parts"; (7) "Fencing in a corner of the hall for those emergencies that are constantly occurring in hospitable families"; (8) "What a paradise could be made in one corner of the sitting-room for the little folks!"

Because screens are nothing more than hinged panels, making them yourself is not difficult. They don't have to be decorated with oriental lacquer or fancy needlework. They are an excellent opportunity to echo some of the textiles, wallpapers, tiles, or stencils featured elsewhere in the room. Gardner also mentioned an arrangement of dried grasses and flowers pressed under glass as a feature that could be incorporated.

Gardner cited an example of a screen used "to hide the refrigerator in the dining room." Along the same lines, a Victorian Revival screen might be used in the living room to hide the large-screen TV and in the bedroom to conceal the exercise equipment.

In 1878, Clarence Cook wrote in The House Beautiful the following comments about screens: "The long, narrow parlors that are such an affliction to New York housekeepers are much more elegantly divided by screens, which may be made as rich or plain as we choose, or by curtains, than by the ordinary partition and sliding door."

SILVERWARE

In the field of Victorian antiques, Victorian silverware—especially American Victorian silverware—has been the most neglected. Yet for those who can set aside their lingering Colonial Revival Paul Revere prejudices, it is an excellent index to the history of Victorian society and style.

Victorian silverware began as an old-fashioned craft that perpetuated eighteenth-century traditional designs for the elite and grew into a nineteenth-century mechanized industry that offered modern designs for the multitude. The history of the Gorham Company of Providence, Rhode Island, summarizes the evolution of American Victorian silverware. In the 1830s Jabez Gorham was painstakingly

hand-hammering silver spoons from old coins and slowly peddling them around New England. Like other makers of coin silver flatware, he made them thin to get the cost down to the point that more people could substitute them for their best pewter spoons. Gorham's handmade spoons came to an end in 1852 when his son John Gorham installed the first steam-powered drop press, which changed a workman's output from one spoon to dozens per hour. By the 1890s Gorham flatware and hollowware were being sold at middle-class prices throughout the United States by Gorham salesmen backed by vigorous advertising. Today, Gorham is the world's largest manufacturer of sterling silverware.

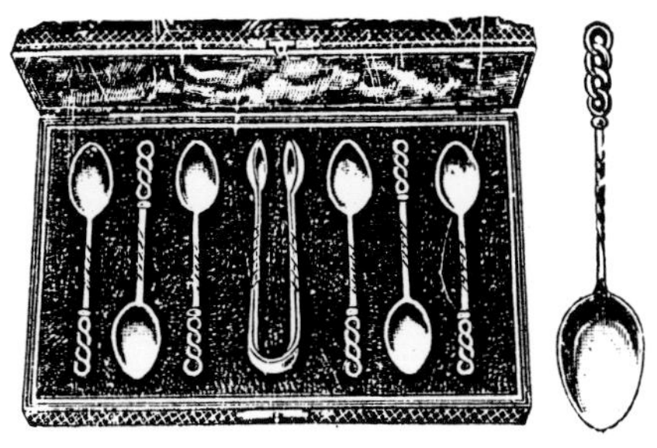

Victorian presentation silver pieces were impressive works. Gorham's famous Century Vase for the 1876 Centennial weighed in at 2000 ounces and was valued at $25,000. It was a miniature yet highly detailed version of grand civic sculpture packed with patriotic symbolism. Other types of Victorian silverware created by Gorham include extravagant table centerpieces called epergnes, highly wrought tea services, punch bowls, and souvenir spoons. Despite the complexity of Gorham's art silverware, the company's 169 flatware patterns, from Fiddle of 1831 to Marguerite of 1901, are the best index of popular Victorian taste.

Late Victorian flatware services mirrored the expanding complexity and elaboration of formal dining, which continues to amuse and disgust late twentieth-century devotees of lean cuisine. By the 1880s, flatware was no longer a simple matter of knife, spoon, and fork. There were spoons, ladles, knives, and forks especially designed for every conceivable use: tea, dessert, salt, mustard, coffee, eggs, sugar, berries, gravy, nuts, salads, ice cream, jelly, preserves, pickles, oysters, fish, pastry, fruit, butter, cake, pie, soup, cream, punch, ice, and asparagus. As if to remind us of those good old days when wonderfully textured, home-baked breads and sponge breads were commonplace, generously served, and enthusiastically consumed, every sociable Victorian home had a silver crumb knife.

Further Reading: Carpenter, Charles H. Jr. *Gorham Silver* (New York: Dodd, Mead, 1982).

SIN

Sin did not take a Victorian holiday despite the intense efforts of Victorian moralists to suppress human nature.

Today's weaponry makes Victorian homicide primitive by comparison, but Victorians were as fascinated as we are by the detection, capture, trial, and punishment of murderers like Jack the Ripper in Britain—who was never captured—and Lizzie Borden in the United States, who gave her mother and father "forty whacks" each with an axe. Sir Arthur Conan Doyle created Sherlock Holmes—the world's most famous fictional detective—in 1887 with the publication of *A Study in Scarlet.* Such subject matter still fascinates people. A recent development in America is the murder-mystery weekend, often held in Victorian bed and breakfast inns.

This prostitute lounges with a strange bedfellow.

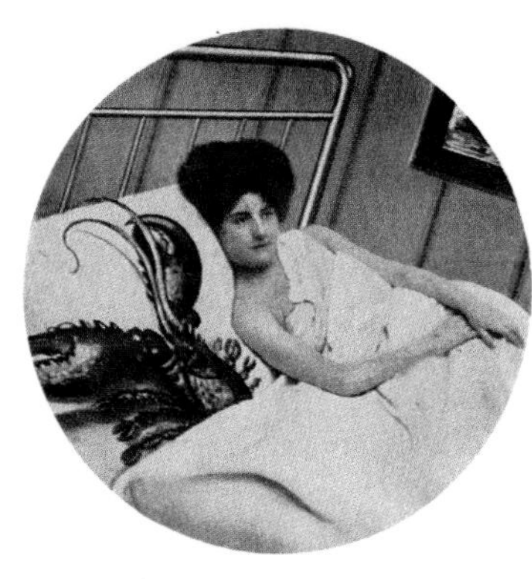

Prostitution during much of the nineteenth century in Britain was state regulated to control the spread of venereal disease, but a prohibition movement of the 1880s put an end to the system, with

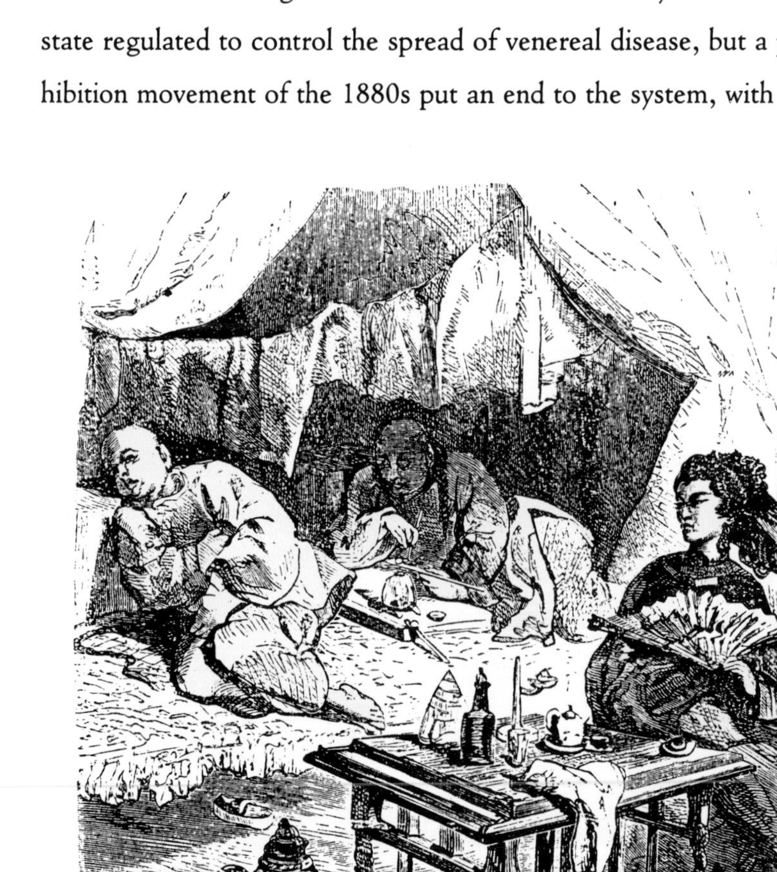

Opium dens were dark, mysterious havens of sin in San Francisco, New York, and other cities. This illustration, from a book on China, shows these men helpless to the allure of opium and the den's female keeper.

For women, cigarette smoking was sin enough.

predictable results. Most peculiar was the evangelism of Prime Minister Gladstone who tried to convert London prostitutes by holding moralizing evening chats and serving hot drinks at home with Mrs. Gladstone. Railway men in the Western United States contributed the term "Red Light District" by parking their kerosene railway lanterns with their red glass chimneys outside brothels conveniently located near the railroad yards.

Souvenirs and Tourism

Making the Grand Tour of Italy, Greece, and Asia Minor—with inevitable souvenir hunting along the way—was the highest ambition of eighteenth-century European and American gentry, but not until a Victorian genius named Thomas Cook invented the railway and steamship excursion did the middle class become tourists.

Cook shepherded 165,000 visitors to and from the Crystal Palace Exhibition of 1851 in London, repeated this feat for the Exhibition in Paris of 1855, and in 1856 began the circular tour of Europe. Cook's first tours were personally conducted, but by the early 1860s he concentrated on the more familiar form of travel agent who sells tickets.

The earliest photographs of Victorian tourists in Europe are pictures of well-padded ladies and gentlemen standing on a Swiss glacier gazing at an Alp. Switzerland was the first European country that could be safely traversed by independent tourists. By 1865 most of Europe was likewise accessible. Cook's Tours to the United States followed in 1866 after the Civil War, but it was the attraction of the 1876 Centennial in Philadelphia that drew the first large crowds of foreign tourists.

Most families possess at least one or two Victorian souvenirs. My favorite is a printed cotton kerchief illustrating the Centennial Exhibition buildings. My great-grandfather brought it back from Philadelphia to my great-grandmother who was pregnant. That's how I remember that my grandmother was born in 1876.

Statuary

The obligatory stone for villa and mansion statuary, which included imported Italian mantels with carved figures, was Carrara marble. The chilling whiteness of Carrara confirmed the erroneous assumption that Greek statuary was originally gleaming white, when in fact it was painted to look like waxwork effigies. This false association was perpetuated by mass-produced, white, translucent, unglazed, molded porcelain figurines called *Parian,* or statuary ware.

When statuary could be turned to practical use, as in cast-iron fountains and garden ornaments, Victorians relaxed their censure. The branching candle arms of girandoles, a fashionable three-piece garniture for shelves of middle-class Early Victorian fireplace mantels, were supported by figural groups set atop marble bases. Popular subjects included Uncle Tom and Eva, Highland Mary, and Jenny Lind—the "Swedish Nightingale," who toured extensively under P.T. Barnum's management on singing engagements. The

Indoor landscape and statuary enliven the central courtyard of the Isabella Stewart Gardner Museum in Boston, Massachusetts.

Jenny Lind motif suggests the girandole's specialized use on pianos to provide light for sheet music. The most pretentious kerosene parlor lamps were distinguished by seminude statues of Greco-Roman women and Renaissance putti. Gasoliers, especially those affixed to the tops of villa and mansion hallway newel posts, invariably sprouted from the outstretched arm of a Gothic warrior in battle dress or a scantily clad Greek or Roman god or goddess.

Most proper Victorians preferred sentimental, anecdotal, and genre statuary decently clothed. The most popular of the type was the Late Victorian Rogers Groups. Staffordshire potteries supplied popular ceramic statuary for Victorian cottages, so much so that collectors used to call them Staffordshire cottage figures. Shaggy-haired dogs are the most famous Staffordshire cottage figures, but the bulk of production were historical figures like Lord Nelson, the Duke of Wellington, Benjamin Franklin, Abraham Lincoln, Queen Victoria, and Prince Albert.

STENCILING

Victorian decorative painters routinely used stencils for repetitive large-scale work. For the purpose, they employed thin metal stencils made by first etching the design and finishing the cutting with an engraver's burin. Smaller-scale, less repetitive work used waxed rag or kraft fiber paper with patterns cut out by a sharp knife. Victorians stenciled a range of flat surfaces, including handkerchiefs, linens, window glass, roller shades, walls, ceilings, floors, floor cloths, boxes, and calling cards.

Imitating ground glass is one technique rarely seen today because it uses the reverse section of the stencil—the part that is cut out. Completely cover one side of the cutout with thin paste and carefully stick it to the glass with every part well pressed down. Use the end of a stencil brush dipped in thick white paint to pounce, or stipple, the glass all over. When dry, raise the paper by putting the blade of a knife under it, and the figure will be found clearly defined on the glass. Border the glass with lines or stripes easily made by scraping through the white paint with a stick drawn along a rule.

Stencil-like patterns have been used in the decoration of the Lund House in East Blue Hill, Maine.

Before you apply the first stencil to a wall, paint three horizontal areas in three harmonious colors to break the wall into a Late Victorian dado, fill, and frieze. Alternatively, paint vertical areas of two colors to break the wall into Early Victorian panels. You can also outline the areas for moldings or borders with masking tape and painted with contrasting or darker colors. Then the stencil patterns can be positioned within these areas.

Early Victorian panels can be decorated with a corner stencil. Use it once in each corner in one color and repeat it four times in the center of the panel in another color to create a star. The same technique can be used in the same or different colors on roller shades. (*See also Roller Shades*)

Taxidermy

Few things conjure up the Victorian period more powerfully yet unfairly than authentic stuffed animals. Taxidermy was an old and popular art before it evolved to a Victorian plateau of perfection in the 1880s, primarily in America under the direction of the Ward Scientific Company, which continues to thrive in Rochester, New York. At the highest level, taxidermy contributed to a biological understanding of animals—of special interest to Victorians after the publication of Charles Darwin's *On the Origin of Species* in 1859. At lower levels it fostered the image of man as hunter. This division between taxidermy for natural history collections and that for the hunter's den exists to this day.

During the course of an excellent luncheon of Scottish salmon caught that morning on the Gothic Revival estate of an Ayrshire laird, I said that many Scottish aristocrats had gone to North America as colonial administrators and asked my host if any of his family had done so. He clouded over and thought hard for a moment, then gaily shouted: "Had a Victorian uncle. Went out to Canada. Shot a moose. Show it to you after lunch." He did. It was in the basement, ratty and covered with dust.

If you find in somebody's attic or basement a stuffed bird or beast in good condition that can be had cheap, consider dusting it off and reinstating it in the curiosity corner of your Victorian parlor. (*See also Dining Room*)

A man's office or study in the Victorian Revival style is the most appropriate place today for stuffed animals. Note the decorative use of rugs and carpets, both over and under the furniture.

TILES

The twentieth century has been so blind to the decorative arts of the Victorian period that it was possible as late as the 1960s to publish a general history of tiles without citing nineteenth-century examples. Yet any discussion of Victorian architecture would be incomplete if it ignored tiles, especially English encaustic tiles, which were promoted in the United States beginning in the 1850s by color-plate advertising pages in stylebooks like Calvert Vaux's *Villas and Cottages* of 1857.

Charles Locke Eastlake's *Hints on Household Taste* (1868) did more than any other book to promote the export of English encaus-

Louis Sullivan, who was a superb Late Victorian designer of architectural ornament, perpetuated his Victorian affection for decorative tiles in his famous early twentieth-century banks.

tic tiles. Minton tiles were duly noted, but an accolade was given to Maw. "For rich variety of pattern, and for the skill with which the best types of ornament have been adapted for enamelled ware, plain tile pavements, mosaic and mural decoration, Messrs. Maw & Co., of Salop, stand almost unrivalled." *Hints* included a dozen color illustrations of Maw encaustic tile pavements and borders.

Eastlake restricted his recommendation of encaustic tiles to the floors of heavy-traffic areas like halls and vestibules. But, like so much of what Eastlake said, it was ignored by enthusiastic Victorians converted to the new religion of art better known as the Aesthetic Movement. Encaustic, majolica, and enameled tiles crept up the walls and migrated into rooms other than halls and vestibules. They were also used in such diverse places as "Wall Linings,

Some of the best surviving examples of Victorian flat pattern in original colors are encaustic tiles, like these "tile pavements" from a catalogue published by Maw.

Dadoes, Friezes, String Courses, Fire Places, etc.," according to a Maw catalogue. It is so packed with richly colored pattern that it looks like Owen Jones's famous 1856 *Grammar of Ornament* brought to life.

Those who study Victorian interior and exterior colors lament the fugitive and altered colors of the paints, wallpapers, and textiles they analyze. The greatest permanent record of Victorian colors lies patiently waiting in Victorian tiles.

Trees

Victorians inherited their devotion to trees in the landscape from eighteenth-century landscape gardening, but we inherited ours from them. They invented Arbor Day, which is alive and well in many places. They taught us to love forests and protect vast acreages of trees. They educated us in the importance of trees in the domestic landscape and tree-lined streets to the extent that contemporary subdivisions never appear comfortably settled until nestled into shade trees.

Andrew Jackson Downing called towns and villages without shade trees "naked"—places "where rude and uncouth streets bask in the summer heat, and revel in the noontide glare, with scarcely a leaf to shelter or break the painful monotony!" No one can be a Victorian lover and remain indifferent to the naked landscapes of cities and suburbs, acid rain, and the plight of the world's rain forests. Nor can they regard with equanimity the disappearance of

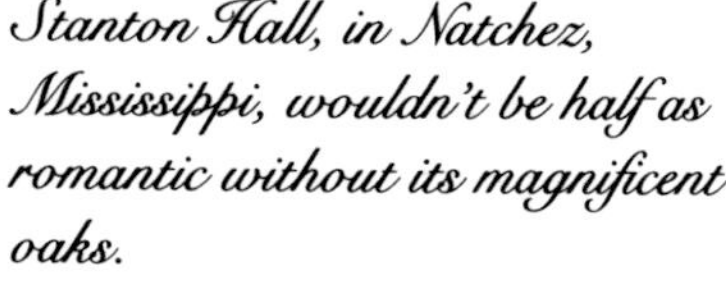

Stanton Hall, in Natchez, Mississippi, wouldn't be half as romantic without its magnificent oaks.

chestnuts and elms, which are currently being revived in disease-resistant varieties.

In his February 1851 *Horticulture* essay on "The Beautiful in a Tree" Downing condemned the insensitive pruning of trees in the domestic landscape, especially trimming the lower branches off to

We hope that enough of these American elms will survive to remind future generations what America's favorite shade tree looked like.

create "a bare pole with a top of foliage at the end of it." Many homeowners today who prune their trees and shrubs do so by hacking at the plants. According to a recent issue of *Horticulture* (August 1990) Cass Turnbull—a latter-day Downing—founded PlantAmnesty in 1987 to focus public attention on murderous pruning and teach proper pruning techniques.

Victorians succeeded in teaching us to perceive and combine trees artistically in the landscape as abstract shapes, but their poetic sensitivity to trees is largely lost. Victorian sentimentality is calling an old apple tree motherly or a magnolia voluptuous, like Frank J. Scott did in his 1870 *Art of Beautifying Suburban Home Grounds*. Scott's description of trees reveals the Victorian's genteel penchant for stating practical matters in elegant terms: "There are trees (like those women who, though brilliant in drawing-rooms, are never less than ladies when busy in domestic labors) which are useful and profitable in orchard and forest, but are doubly beautiful in robes of greater luxuriance upon the carpet of a rich lawn. There are others which no care in culture will make ornaments in 'the best society.' "

Sources: PlantAmnesty, 906 NW 87th St., Seattle, WA, 98117. This five-hundred-member group offers a video and pamphlet on tree-pruning techniques.

Trellis

Perhaps the most neglected aspect of Victorian exterior decoration is the art of trellising—diverse kinds of latticed framework or ladders designed to support climbing vines. Victorians used flowering vines to strengthen and beautify blank or unattractive areas. An 1857 design from Calvert Vaux's *Villas and Cottages* shows a simple ladder trellis decorating a blank space on the side of a house. The verandah, with the exception of simple brackets in the corners where the cornice meets the supports, consists entirely of latticed trellis.

Owners of the plainer varieties of Early Victorian homes lament their lack of architectural detail in comparison with highly ornate Late Victorian homes. When a Victorian home lacked architectural detail, it was given horticultural detail with trelliswork.

Like other practical and beautiful aspects of Victorian decoration, the trellis has been neglected because it is not carefree. Vines have to be cut back after the killing frosts and pruned in the spring. Lattice and ladders are an additional and difficult maintenance item. But they are worth the effort because they bring dead areas to life even when the vines have been cut back. Victorian trellis designs, like those from an 1881 architectural detail book, were decorative in their own right and painted in positive colors to harmonize or contrast with the colors of the walls behind them.

A simple, flat-arched trellis focuses the eye in the gardens of Lyndhurst at Tarrytown, New York.

Vines can beautify and cool areas, but without a well-maintained trellis they can destroy surfaces by attachment, infiltration, and mildew. A trellis positioned away from walls discourages these conditions from developing and is healthy for both the house and the vines.

For those who dislike permanent trellises, A.J. Downing supplies a solution in his February 1849 *Horticulture* essay "On the Drapery of Cottages and Gardens." In the essay he reported a Belgian invention for urban Victorians "who have neither cottages nor gardens—who are confined to a little front and backyard of a town life." The Trellis Mobile "is a strong wooden box, upon wooden rollers about three feet long and the double trellis eight or ten feet high. In this box the finer sorts of exotic climbers, such as passion flowers, everblooming roses, maurandias, ipomea learii may be grown with charming effect." During colder weather the device could be brought indoors.

A trellis ceiling creates one of the most pleasant of outdoor areas.

UNDERCLOTHES

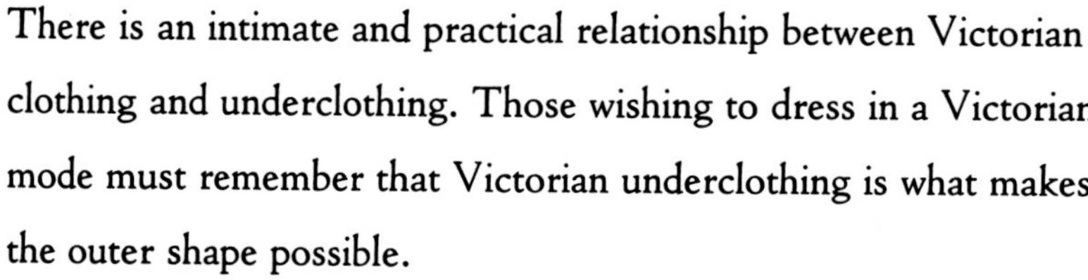

There is an intimate and practical relationship between Victorian clothing and underclothing. Those wishing to dress in a Victorian mode must remember that Victorian underclothing is what makes the outer shape possible.

Victorian women, alas, were the major victims of torturous and cumbersome underclothes, which redistributed gender specific parts of their anatomy or amplified what genetics had failed to supply. Victorian underclothes were like Victorian architecture; past traditions were revived and technologically improved. The best example is the crinoline, invented in 1856 as a lightweight improvement on the eighteenth-century hoop skirt and substitute for a platoon of early nineteenth-century petticoats. It was called an *artificial crinoline, cage petticoat,* or *cage crinoline.* Bustles and corsets existed long before their use during the Victorian period, including the male use of corsets by Regency dandies and Beau Brummell swells. In the 1840s a tailored undervest called a "waistcoat," better known as the camisole, was developed to cover a lady's corset.

Individuals have been associated with certain underclothes, but only one has been remembered. In 1849 an American lady in Seneca Falls, New York, named Amelia Bloomer transformed the late eighteenth-century pantaloon or Victorian "pantalette," which extended down the legs below the calf, into Turkish trousers tied at the ankles. Although practical and comfortable, these loose trousers were ridiculed out of existence for their associations with Early Victorian feminism. They were quietly revived in the late 1890s to make it possible for women to participate in the bicycle craze.

The vogue for cleanliness expressed in terms of underclothes was not a Victorian creation and had more to do with social distinction than sanitary living. In the late eighteenth century, Beau Brummell made clean linen the touchstone of gentility: "no perfumes, but very fine linen, plenty of it, and country washing." This survived into the twentieth century and was practiced by people like Jimmy "Beau James" Walker, the gentleman mayor of New York City in the late

1920s famous for changing his clothes four or five times a day. The concept is still alive and well in the recent antiperspirant slogan, "Never let them see you sweat."

Incidently, to satisfy curiosity, it should be mentioned that the brassiere was not invented and named until the early twentieth century, and women did not wear drawers or underpants until the nineteenth century, drawers being a form of male underclothing. Sarah Josepha Hale, the editor of *Godey's Ladys' Book,* is the one who popularized the term lingerie.

Further Reading: Cunnington, C. Willet and Phyllis. *The History of Underclothes (London: Michael Joseph, 1951).*

UPHOLSTERY

A history of Victorian furniture could be written exclusively on the changing relationship of exposed framing and upholstery. No decorative technique better sums up the Victorian love of comfort and class consciousness than upholstery. Victorians loved upholstered women, upholstered flowers, upholstered gardens, upholstered architectural detailing, as well as upholstered furniture.

Prior to the invention of mechanized carving machines, the only way Late Victorian furniture manufacturers like those based in Grand Rapids, Michigan, could make cheap furniture retaining the luxurious associations of genteel Early Victorian design was to cover it entirely with upholstery. This disguised the cheap framing and avoided expensive hand-carving.

Perhaps the Victorian version of a daybed called a lounge but better known today as a "fainting couch" is the most typical exam-

This lavish upholstered piece of furniture is a beautiful example of a "double-pouffe ottoman."

ple of Victorian upholstery, but the ottoman runs a close second. Obviously derived from Turkish sources, it was made popular by the naughty literary romanticism of Byron's *Don Juan.* In its homeland it was a low pile of plump pillows, but Early Victorians transformed it into a low cushioned seat set into a recess to accommodate

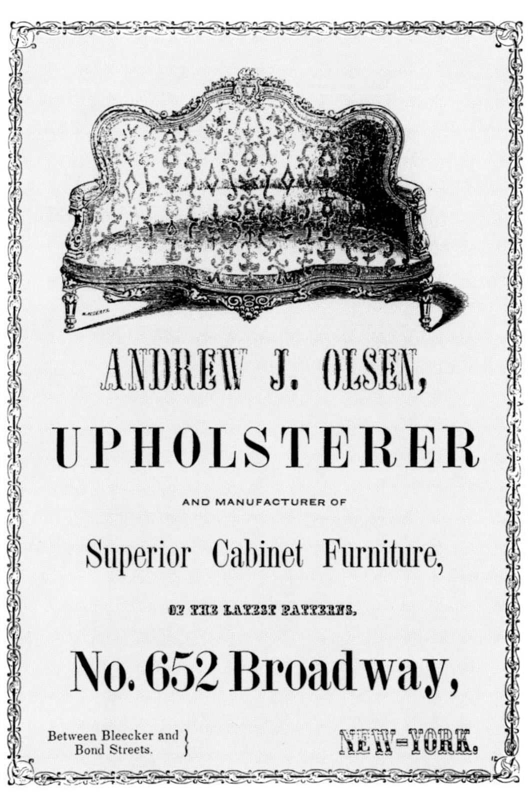

three or four persons. The most luxurious kind of ottoman was a richly upholstered circular seat with a hub supporting a display of flowers or sculpture. It was usually set in the middle of a large parlor or drawing room. By the time *The Practical Upholsterer* was published in 1891, the ottoman had dwindled to a pair of upholstered square frames placed at forty-five degree angles to each other and set near to the floor. It looked more like a footstool, but the "double-pouffe ottoman" was actually closer to the piled pillows of the Turkish prototype.

Valances and Lambrequins

Victorian valances had the same relationship to whatever they appeared to cover indoors as Victorian brackets had to whatever they appeared to support outdoors. They had no structural function and were entirely decorative. Today, the term valance is restricted

The ruffle between the curtains in this nursery is a simple valance, "easy to cut," used to finish the window space.

to a horizontal band of straight, pleated, or swagged textile with straight or scalloped bottom edges hung vertically from a rod, track, or shelf over the top of the drapes. In the United States during the Victorian period the concept was extended to any ornate textile cornice and called a lambrequin. A fireplace mantel shelf, bookshelf, and a small table placed against the wall to display an important object were prime candidates for a lambrequin exhibiting all the ornamental needlework skills of the lady of the house.

Modern devices make it possible for amateur decorators to emulate some of the more simple swags and pleats without complicated cutting. But more complex and elaborate Victorian valances require a professional upholsterer. That is why *The Practical Upholsterer* (1891) recommended straight valances for amateurs, because "they are easy to cut."

Placing a valance above a short window increases their apparent height while blocking little of the light. Of course, any valance must be scaled and proportioned to the window area.

VALENTINES

The acme of popular Victorian printing, embossing, and collage was the valentine. It mixed and matched an astonishing array of materials, including the following: silk fringe, jacquard woven silk, velvet flowers, clusters of pearls, mirrors, embossed silver paper, gold lace paper, hand-tinted prints, moss, satin ribbons, gilded wire, tinsel, cambric flowers, glass beads, and feathers.

Lace paper, upon which many Victorian valentines depended, was an innovation discovered by accident when an embossed sheet of paper stuck to the male die in the press and got the thinned tops of the embossing filed away. Charles Dickens describes the deliberate procedure developed from it in the February 20, 1864 issue of *All the Year Round,* a weekly journal he edited, under the title of "Cupid's Manufactory." It is a thinly disguised account of Joseph Mansell's factory in London. After a run of paper is embossed, the male die is removed from the press and individual embossed sheets are repositioned, "adjusting it exactly by means of regulating pins at the corners, and then with flat iron tools covered with fine sand-paper, the projecting bosses on the paper are rubbed off."

The greatest American success story involving valentines is that of Esther Howland, daughter of a Worcester, Massachusetts, stationer and bookseller. After graduating from Mount Holyoke College in 1847, she made her first collage valentines the following year on Mansell lace paper. Her inventive artistry eventually translated into annual sales of $100,000.

The beauty and profusion of Victorian valentines never signified proper Victorian approval of them. Emily Dickinson, reporting to her brother February 14, 1848, from Mount Holyoke College after Esther Howland had sold her first $5,000 worth of valentines, wrote: "Monday afternoon Mistress Lyon arose in the hall and forbade our sending any of those foolish notes called valentines."

Further Reading: Lee, Ruth Webb. *A History of Valentines* (New York: 1952). Staff, Frank. *The Valentine & Its Origins* (New York: Praeger, 1969).

Verandahs and Porches

Current architectural parlance lumps porches and verandahs together. Although they frequently were parts of the same facade, to Victorian architects like Calert Vaux they were distinct architectural features. Vaux's 1857 stylebook titled *Villas and Cottages* called a *porch* or *entrance* the first part of a design "that appeals to the attention of a visitor, and admits of much character and expression." It hailed the *verandah* as "perhaps the most specially American feature in a country house, and nothing can compensate for its absence."

A great verandah is a year-round joy, even after a snowstorm.

Vaux provides the clue to separate porches from verandahs in his mention of a porch as an entrance. Porches are sheltered areas in front of entrances. Verandahs are sheltered areas in front of walls. When combined, the porch is often distinguished from the verandah by having a gable set at a right angle to the shed roof of the verandah. When they were combined on the side of a house without benefit of a gable, Vaux called the feature a verandah-porch.

For smaller cottages Vaux recommended over-scaling and boldly projecting a porch eight to ten feet as a surrogate verandah, which "may be fitted with glazed frames and an outer door for winter use." An alternative was an enclosed porch that functioned as an externalized vestibule.

No exterior feature of Victorian domestic architecture has suffered more than the verandah. It has been the victim of neglect caused by a radical change in social values beginning in the 1920s, when verandahs moved from the facades of homes, migrated to the side walls, and became enclosed as breakfast rooms, sun rooms, sun porches, and solariums.

Verandahs were a key architectural element in Victorian socializing. Residents of the house, sitting on the verandah, would wave a hand or call hello to someone passing by in the street or along the sidewalk; their invitation would progress through a request to "sit a spell," with or without refreshments depending upon the climate and time of day, to an impromptu invitation for tea or supper.

Verandahs were places where Victorians could escape the formalities of entrance, hallway, parlor, or dining room and be themselves. Children could romp and play to their heart's content without making their parents nervous about the security of the decor, especially during rainy weather. Exposed to public view, young couples could talk to each other without chaperons. Adults could relax and socialize with whomever they chose without having to invite them indoors. During hot weather, the verandah served as a cool refuge, especially while the family waited for the house to cool down in the evening.

Why stop a good thing? The first-floor verandah in this Key West, Florida, house has been echoed in its second-floor balcony.

Victuals

The bulk of what Victorians ate is what is now called "comfort food"—unpretentious, good-tasting food in season. There is much to envy: unpolluted streams, rivers, estuaries, and shorelines were crowded with crustaceans and fish; the skies were filled with fowl instead of foul air. Victorian festive foods like terrapin and canvasback duck are no longer available in quantity. To complicate matters further, we are anxious about the hidden dangers of our meat, fish, grains, and vegetables.

Today's problem is that most people are so detached from the growing of their food they have forgotten that taste is in the mouth and not the eye, best symbolized by that battleship fruit of modern commerce, the Red Delicious apple. Victorian fruits were superficially described to identify them, but what really mattered to Victorians was how they tasted, what they were best used for, and how well they stored.

An excellent Victorian meal might consist of a soup course made from your own stock, your own unsweetened bread or muffins, a crown roast of pork, reverently prepared vegetables from your garden, an elegantly simple salad, homemade ice cream or sherbet, and superb coffee or tea carefully brewed. Any of your own preserves, pickles, and relishes would further honor your table. Homemade applesauce, tomato aspic, and sauerkraut relish would complement the pork. If you prefer beer to wine, don't let today's wine mystique stop you; make it a special one from a micro-brewery matched to the meal. Afterwards, in the parlor serve fresh fruits, cheese, and a port, madiera, or sauterne.

Further Reading: Freeman, John Crosby. *Victorian Entertaining* (Philadelphia: Running Press, 1989).

Wallpaper

"My wallpaper is killing me, one of us must go" was the final witticism of Oscar Wilde before he died in 1900 in the Hotel d'Alsace, Paris. Wilde wasn't the only Victorian jeopardized by wallpaper. Clarence Cook's famous pamphlet published in New York in 1880 asked, "What Shall We Do With Our Walls?" Those who answered "wallpaper" ran the risk of decorative mayhem. The enormous quantity and variety of seductive-looking and attractively priced wallpapers generated by Victorian technology made it difficult to select papers with appropriate colors, patterns, and scale.

Victorian guidebooks repeated such common-sense wisdom as: (1) avoid large-scale patterns and dark colors for small rooms because they make them look smaller; (2) use vertical stripes to make a small room look larger, "but where the stripes are too decided, the appearance is that of a room barred in"; (3) do not use floral wallpaper in rooms in which many pictures are to be hung.

This room is a stunning example of the handcrafted reproduction wallcoverings available from Bradbury & Bradbury of Benicia, California.

Professional decorators and homeowners with taste followed such advice, but Victorian photographs reveal wallpapered interiors that broke these rules.

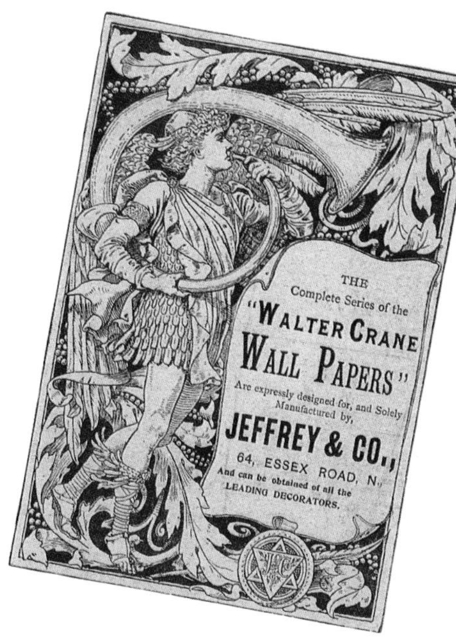

Victorian craftsmen who installed wallpaper were called paper hangers—a name that preserved the original association of wallpaper, or paper tapestries, as a substitute for woven wall hangings. Victorian wallpapers were made to look like other surfaces, including wood wainscots and panels, gilded and embossed leather, and masonry blocks. The majority of them, however, imitated textiles, especially medieval flocked wool, Renaissance silk and velvet, Elizabethan embroidery, and baroque damask. Calico printing provided the concept of repeating designs, but wallpaper manufacturers didn't have continuous lengths of paper until the web or fourdrinier paper-making machine was developed at the beginning of the nineteenth century. The first machine, or roller-printed, papers weren't made until 1840, shortly after Britain removed a burdensome excise tax in 1836.

Two special categories were panoramic papers imitating painted murals, at which the French excelled from the beginning of the nineteenth century and Early Victorian architecturally framed scenes. The former were too expensive for anyone but the wealthy. The latter were ridiculed out of existence by architects like Pugin and decorative designers like Owen Jones, Charles Eastlake, and William Morris, whose efforts were focused on designing patterns honoring the reality of wallpaper's flat surface.

The four most popular Victorian styles of wallpaper placement were: (1) single repeated design from baseboard to ceiling; (2) top-of-the-wall border; (3) panels; (4) dado-fill-frieze. Due to recent enthusiasm for Late Victorian Queen Anne decoration, dado-fill-frieze has become the quintessential style of the Victorian Revival. Other varieties should be explored, such as, combining wallpaper with painting, glazing, and stencilling.

General color sentiments associated with different areas of a house also pertained to wallpaper. (*See also Color: Interior*) The most important verdict governing the selection of wallpaper is the same as that for carpets and rugs—deciding which elements should be emphasized. Should the wallpaper be an attractive background for the accessories of a room, or should it be featured as a design element? Victorians were concerned about how wallpapers would "light up" under candle, gas, or kerosene lighting. Artificial illumination is presently available from cool to warm. Select your lighting before you select your wallpapers, and see how a sample looks under this light before you order it.

Further Reading: "Historic Wallcoverings," a 1990 listing available from *Traditional Building,* 79-A Seventh Ave., Brooklyn, NY 11217. Nylander, Richard C. *Wall Papers for Historic Buildings, A Guide to Selecting Reproduction Wallpapers* (Washington, D.C.: Preservation Press, 1983). *The Paper Hanger, Painter, Grainer, and Decorator's Assistant,* a reprint of an 1879 London guidebook available from American Life Books, PO Box 349, Watkins Glen, NY 14891. *Wallpaper Reproduction News,* available by subscription from Robert M. Kelly, PO Box 187, Lee, MA 01238.

Beautiful Victorian Revival wallcoverings are offered by Brunschwig & Fils.

WEDDINGS

Victorians were romantics, and they especially excelled at creating elegant, charming weddings. The Victorian wedding is especially viable today because it strikes a chord of originality at a time when most aspects of contemporary weddings have been manufactured, prepackaged, and otherwise commercialized by the suppliers of wedding services. Victorian weddings also give couples and their

families historical rationale for avoiding the financial ruin of contemporary weddings. Victorians revered the institution of marriage above all others, but they feared bankruptcy even more. Despite the gargantuan society weddings of the late nineteenth century, most Victorian weddings were simple and genteel, but highly romantic affairs.

Victorian theme weddings simplify nearly every aspect of the event. Wedding dresses often were designed and made by brides so they could be used for subsequent entertainments. Many brides were married in traveling dresses because they literally had a train to catch. Flowers used at the ceremony and reception were in season, which is why most weddings were scheduled for June, when the supply was at its height. Furthermore, because Victorians used a

symbolic language of the flowers, wedding flowers were selected for personal meanings, which made them more enjoyable. (*See also Language of the Flowers*) Weddings often took place at home, something that can be emulated today by booking a Victorian bed and breakfast inn for the event. Nineteenth-century wedding breakfasts were actually elegant luncheons.

The single common element of Victorian and contemporary weddings is the wedding cake. The massive, tiered, richly decorated wedding cake is the one Victorian wedding tradition that continued to thrive in the twentieth century.

Further Reading: St. Marie, Satig, and Flaherty, Carolyn. *The Victorian Wedding—Then and Now: Bringing the Romantic Past to Life* (New York: E.P. Dutton, 1991).

Window Casings

Interior window casings—the framework that holds the sash—are often obscured by drapes. If your interior casings are too good to cover up, consider achieving privacy and softening the glare of sunlight with interior blinds, inset lace panels, decorated roller shades, or "sheers," which were called "glass curtains" or "window curtains" in the Victorian era.

Outside windows often look strange today because the house has lost its shutters and exterior blinds when they became useless after the installation of aluminum storm windows and air conditioning. To accommodate shutters and blinds, the sides or faces of window casings were often left blank or, in the instance of brick buildings, left off altogether. When they are removed, the window becomes a disconnected sill and lintel weakly linked by glazed sash. The more ornamental the sash and lintel—especially when the latter has a richly detailed cap or canopy—the barer the window looks. Instead of installing obsolete, expensive, custom-made shutters and blinds—a continual maintenance problem—link the sills and lintels with boards detailed in the style of the house.

Victorian window caps were made in cast-iron, embossed galvanized sheet metal, and terra-cotta as well as wood. If you are creating a Victorian Revival house in one of the less ornate, Early Victorian styles, the addition of a few simple moldings, keystones, drop finials, or brackets can transform an ordinary modern window casing into something special for not much money or effort. Under the sill put an apron and a pair of simple brackets that continue the vertical lines of the casing's side faces.

Window Gardens

Victorian window gardens were also called parlor gardens and winter gardens, the latter because most window gardening took place indoors during the winter. But the term also describes year-round gardens of flowers, ferns, and vines. These could be located near both sides of the window in boxes, or plant stands, hanging baskets, and terrariums.

Most pictures of Victorian window gardens are offputting. They illustrate the common tendency of the period's gardeners to overwhelm the structure of the window with a jungle of plant material—similar to the Victorian practice of obscuring the structure of furniture with upholstery.

Consider a window garden structure that appeared in the September 1895 issue of *Ladies' Home Journal.* A simple, paneled box eighteen inches deep supported by a pair of plain brackets carried to the floor is the base for a wire net lattice with one-inch openings placed between four turned stairway balusters to create side panels connected across the front by a top spandrel. The tops of two small boxes placed perpendicular to the window are positioned on the inside of the side panels so they line up with the top of the lower window sash.

To create an attractive window garden, be sure that your window box or plant container is in proportion to the window. If it is an

Window garden designs from Vick's Flower and Vegetable Garden.

indoor box or container, be sure that its coloration either matches or harmonizes with the interior walls and woodwork. This will ensure that your window garden complements the architecture of the window instead of conquering it. The same principle should prevail when positioning a box outside the window. It is common practice to place a box within the casing on top of the sill, thereby destroying the proportions of the window. The proper method is to hang the box below or in front of the sill and equal in width to the sill, thereby adding depth to the sill and enriching the proportions of the window.

Further Reading: Williams, Henry T. *Window Gardening* (New York: 1871). Walker, Marian C. *Flowering Bulbs for Winter Windows* (Princeton, N.J.: D. Van Nostrand, 1965). Bubel, Nancy "Planting a Window Box," *Horticulture* (June 1988).

Wood Engraving

The most popular form of illustration during the Victorian period was wood engraving, which was significantly cheaper and quicker to produce than steel engraving. Its nearest competitor was lithographs, which had to be printed separate from the text on a special press. Wood engravings could be printed at the same time as the text. This made possible great Victorian illustrated periodicals like *Harper's Weekly* and *Scientific American.*

After the Civil War, American publishing was centered in New York City and therefore so was wood engraving. The best traditions of London wood engraving came to the United States when William James Linton arrived in New York in 1867 at the age of fifty-five. He was an artist, chief engraver for the *Illustrated London News,* essayist, political activist, and teacher of pupils like the great Aesthetic Movement artist Walter Crane. In New York, Linton continued his career in teaching, politics, and art.

This wood engraving is from an advertisement, displaying the elaborate possibilities of this interpretive art form.

In the late 1870s the new technology of photography was invading the graphic arts. A younger generation of wood engravers called the New School and led by Timothy Cole transferred photographs of paintings onto wood and minutely engraved the surface to make a facsimile of the work that emulated the fine tonal gradations of photographs. Linton, who was easily dubbed an old conservative, vehemently argued for a return to wood engraving as an art that interpreted images instead of copying them.

Photoengraving, which is still the principal method by which pictures are reproduced on paper, eventually proved Linton right and Cole wrong—but not before it made all styles of wood engraving obsolete. It has survived in the twentieth century in the form in which Linton would approve, as a fine art honored for its special graphic qualities. Contemporary artists using computer graphics might profit from a reverent study of Victorian wood engraving, but perhaps there is no substitute for the discipline of the burin graver pushed through end-grain boxwood.

By contemporary artistic standards, Victorian wood engraving is merely popular illustration and facsimile. For those able to cut through such prejudice, Victorian wood engravings are the cheapest source of real Victorian pictures. As you select and prepare them for your walls, try to follow two rules: (1) Never cut out an engraving from an intact book or magazine; (2) Never color an engraving —it destroys the original integrity of the work.

If you ever wondered about the angular lines in large wood engravings, they are the sides of smaller wood blocks joined to make a large block. It was a method used by Victorian journals to process pictures of current events quickly—especially calamities like fires, railroad wrecks, and sinking ships. The overall picture was drawn on a large block composed of smaller blocks, taken apart, farmed out to many separate engravers who did their part overnight, and reassembled the next day.

Further Reading: Linton, W.J. *The History of Wood-Engraving in America* (Boston: Estes and Lauriat, 1882). Facsimile available from American Life Books, Watkins Glen, NY.

X-RAY

Wilhelm Konrad Roentgen, a German physicist, observed in 1895 the power of cathode rays to pass through opaque substances, fluoresce a specially prepared screen, and affect a photographic plate. Because he was uncertain about the nature of this light, he called it an X-ray. He received the Nobel Prize for physics in 1901.

An illustration from the French news magazine <u>L'Illustration</u>, June 18, 1898.

You-Name-It

Victorian hardware catalogs are filled with mysterious implements and decorative accessories. Here is a selection to test your knowledge of the period and guessing ability. Each artifact is complete in itself. The answers appear on the following page, upside down.

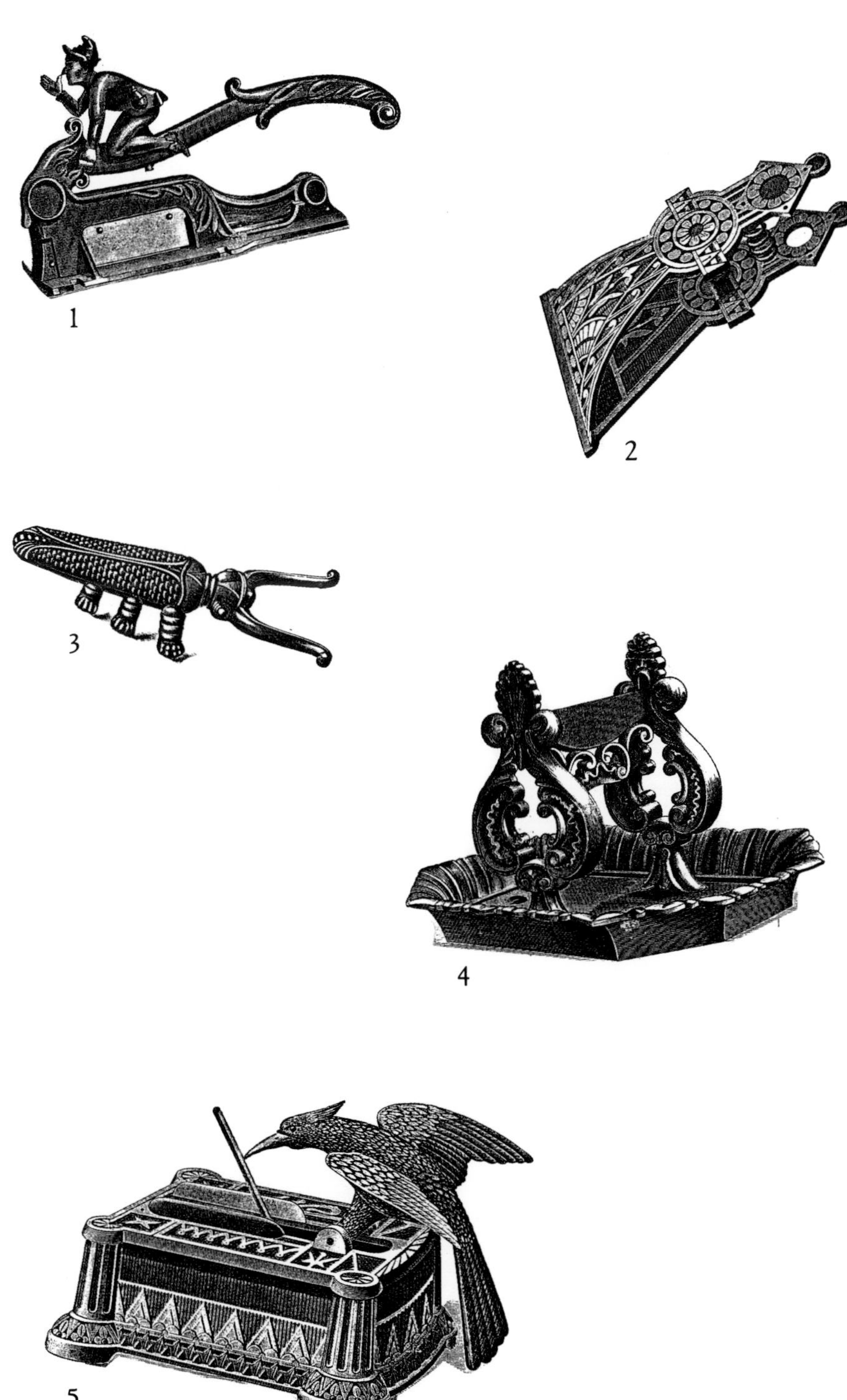

6

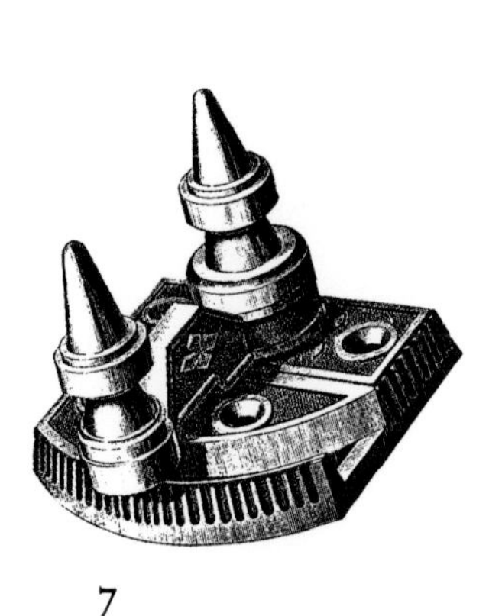

7

8

9

1. Tobacco cutter
2. Paper clip
3. Boot jack
4. Foot scraper
5. Match safe
6. Door bells
7. Burglar-proof sash fastener
8. Chandelier hook
9. Twine box

Zoos

Victorians called them "zoological gardens." They were the descendants of the private menageries of Renaissance and baroque kings and princes. The first one opened to the public in the United States was at Philadelphia in 1874—in time for the 1876 Centennial exhibition in nearby Fairmount Park. The original buildings and entrance were designed by Philadelphia's rogue elephant of architecture, Frank Furness.

PHOTOGRAPHY CREDITS

Art Resource, New York/Tate Gallery; 47, 48
© Gordon Beall; 67
Courtesy of Bradbury & Bradbury Wallpapers; 160
Courtesy of the Cooper-Hewitt Museum, Smithsonian Institution/Art Resource, New York. London, England, c. 1880, Carlo Giuliano, maker. Purchased in memory of Annie Schermerhorn Kane and Susan Dwight Bliss, 1969, photo © John Parnell
© Derek Fell; 147
© Charles Friend; 38, 158
Friends of Olana, Inc.; 15,85,128
© Mark E. Gibson; 26, 30, 33 lower left, 39, 50
© George Goodwin; 46, 100a upper left, 148
© Dennis Gottlieb; 98
© Higgins & Ross; 76, 77 center
© Lee Hocker, from the collection of Phyllis Lapham Ltd., Antiques; 112
© Wolfgang Kaehler; 56
© Lynn Karlin; 13, 74, 75 lower right
© Balthazar Korab; 10, 12, 16, 41, 44, 45, 49, 51, 68, 71, 77 upper right, 84 lower right, 91, 101, 106, 107 left, 109, 115 upper right, 117, 118, 126, 134, 144, 146, 157
© Kenneth Martin/Amstock; 78 top left, 111, 140
© Kent Oppenheimer; 20, 113 lower left, 125, 143
© Edward Owen; 60, 114,162
© Robert Perron; 19 lower left, 25, 29, 66, 83, 116, 142, 149
© Eric Roth; 36
© Bill Rothschild; 52, 152,154
© Shelburne Museum, Shelburne, Vermont; 22, 23, 62, 105, 121, 122
© Tom Tracy; 69
© Brian Vanden Brink; 90, 102 right, 133